«»

I sing for you from this other side of the wall

        You keep hearing your name and recall

That every word I say or every kiss

        It makes you never have to worry or miss

And I keep singing the same old song

        Getting older with a soul quite young

For I never give up the mother tongue

        A word of love, thousand kisses long

«»

EGOLESS LOVE

FIRST EDITION

Hadi Shamsi

This edition is illustrated by Maryam Shamsi.
This edition is proof-read by Hadi Shamsi and Adriana C. Duebel.

First Edition: 2019
Printed in the United States of America.

Library of Congress Control Number: 2019910762
ISBN: 9781099018909

DEDICATION

Humbly dedicated to her.

CONTENTS

CHAPTER ONE

Once strong and limpid as a river, my determination had frozen over with indifference. That unspeakable night had covered everything in an everlasting darkness.

At the time of writing this book, I was a twenty-eight years old male immigrant, living in Houston, Texas. I came to the United States of America as a PhD student in Chemical Engineering. I was not rich, but I was relatively comfortable and so, materialistically speaking, life was good. However, emotionally speaking, I felt a painful vacuum in my life.

It wasn't that I didn't know what I ultimately wanted in my search for happiness. On the contrary, I knew well that true love would bring real happiness into my life. In fact, love had always been the fire in my heart, the voice in my head, and the light in my eyes. Every dream and every star used to be a sign that maybe someday, I would find my one and only love. I had always been a proud romantic, never shy to openly talk about that uplifting essence of love.

There was just a tiny catch: I had been searching for true love for years everywhere I went, but all of that searching had led me to nothing but exhaustion and disappointment. It was as if the more I looked for it, the more it slipped away. In fact, when it came to true love, I had always known myself as a fighter who would never give up, but after that night, it felt like there was nothing to fight for anymore.

I was finally giving up and accepting that maybe I was the aberration. Maybe, others were right when they say true love doesn't exist. Maybe, they were right to see love as a game of musical chairs where the winners are the ones who act faster. Maybe I was overthinking everything.

Trying to come to terms with the idea that the pure love I sought only existed in the stories was killing me from inside out. The events of my life had brought me to this point where I had lost faith in the biggest dream of my life and without it, I was no one—a wandering soul without a purpose.

Those days were, undoubtedly, among my darkest days. I was not just hopeless but pessimistic, bitter, and antisocial. Even when I was not a hermit and actually showed up in a social setting, I would hesitate to make eye contact with anyone or even smile. Avoidance was the name of the game. Even though my solitude and silence weren't really helping the situation, I felt like it would be pointless to talk to people. They would not understand my love and would accuse me of being desperate or melodramatic. I felt safer just keeping all of that pain to myself.

Luckily though, I had few really good friends around me who could understand what I had been through. Especially Sarah, who was one of my best friends. She had noticed that I was withdrawing, and was concerned for me. She kept referring me to different psychologists and psychiatrists. I appreciated her worrying about me, and I had tried a few of them, but nothing helped. I took whatever medications those doctors prescribed, even sat through long therapy sessions that I always hated, but nothing seemed to work.

One day Sarah called me on my phone and told me about a doctor who had a special whole-day therapy program. She said she was visiting her cousins and one of them had told her about how this program had helped him with depression and trauma. Sarah's cousin had told her that this doctor used a special hypnotic technique that was nothing short of a miracle with respect to results. So, like so many times before, Sarah gave me the doctor's name and number and greatly insisted that I should give this doctor and her new technique a chance.

Deep in my heart, I was too pessimistic to talk to yet another shrink, but to appease Sarah, I called that doctor's office one early morning, answered what felt like a ton of questions, and finally scheduled an introductory appointment for a Wednesday, four weeks later.

On the day of appointment, I got to her office at 7:30 am—about thirty minutes before my appointment. I usually hate to be late, even to an appointment I have no desire to attend. The office was located on the first floor of a relatively old two-story brick building, a typical structure in that area of the midtown.

I was admitted at the front desk and was asked to sit there in the lobby until my name was called. Like any other medical office in the United States, they handed me a release and confidentiality form to fill out while I was waiting. The waiting room was typical of a medical office, furnished with a couple of old but comfortable black leather couches and a glass rectangular table in the middle with a variety of health magazines on the top. I sat in the corner of a couch by the old sliding window that was facing the street. After quickly and carelessly filling out the forms, I completely zoned out, which had recently become a habit of mine. Losing track of time in the pleasant universe of absenteeism, I didn't know for how many minutes I was drawn into those thoughts, but suddenly I heard the nurse almost shouting, "Mr. Shamsi! Are you ready for your appointment?"

That day, Houston was getting washed out by one of those heavy sub-tropical showers we got every now and then. While keeping an eye on the street in a tuned out way, I was entranced by those gigantic rain droplets hitting the glass until the nurse's loud call had abruptly disturbed my gaze at the persistent bitterness of that heavy rain.

I slowly and rather reluctantly stood up and followed the

nurse down a narrow corridor to the doctor's office. As we were heading to the doctor's office, negative thoughts were rushing into my mind: *that I was there only because of Sarah's constant prodding, or that I was certain this doctor too would just be yet another quack who couldn't change anything tangible in my life.*

The nurse asked me to take a seat in the office until Dr. Chapman arrived. To my surprise, the room was decorated with fairly comfortable furniture, lots of books on the bookshelf, and some beautiful flowers—nothing like a typical doctor's office. Although I couldn't quite pinpoint the reason, her office had a nice and relaxing flow of energy. After sitting for a minute, I got bored of waiting, so I stood up and walked around a little bit. The room had a covered patio with a view of a little garden in the backyard. It was a really neat garden with different types of exotic plants all arranged in parallel rows. At the end of the yard, one could see a couple of full-grown live oak trees and a pretty fountain in the middle.

Despite the calming effect of the room, I still continued to feel sad and empty. My mind was filled with a somber silence, while my eyes were staring at the garden. I was so isolated in the corner of my own mind that I failed to realize the doctor had already entered the room until she said in a British accent, "Good morning, Mr. Shamsi! Fancy a cuppa?"

Being unaccustomed to British phrases, I didn't quite understand what she meant by "a cuppa," but I answered rather brusquely, "Oh, hey!" She looked like a woman in her early fifties with white hair, but she still had healthy, almost glowing skin. She took her long beige raincoat off and hung it on the hanger near the door. The raincoat was dripping wet, which indicated that she just came in from outside. Underneath that raincoat, she was wearing white pants, white shoes, and a V-neck white shirt with red and green flower patterns around the neck and shoulder. She approached the teapot set on the corner table, and as she was preparing some fresh tea, she said with a calm voice, "Sorry I was a couple of minutes late. I teach an early morning yoga and meditation class in a place downtown."

I nodded my head without saying a word to show I heard her.

I was still standing near the window and maybe she felt uncomfortable with that, because she pointed to the couch near the door and said, "Please! Make yourself comfortable, perhaps on the couch right there."

I slowly walked across the room and sat on the couch near the door again.

It took her a couple of minutes to get settled in the room, and in the meantime, the tea finished brewing. She carefully poured the tea into her cup, added a teaspoon of sugar, and started swirling it gently and noiselessly.

She calmly approached the chair near the couch, sat down, placed the cup on the side table, then looked at me and said, "Very well, let's start talking about the treatment we offer in this office. I'm Dr. Jennifer Chapman, a psychiatrist, certified hypnotherapist, and Jungian analyst. The kind of therapy I am mostly engaged with these recent years, as you may already know, is based on a combination of hermetic and scientific methods. There aren't any known risks involved, but for the sake of full disclosure, this method is not yet widely accepted in the psychiatric community, so some of my colleagues consider it experimental. In practice, you will experience a special form of hypnotic trance, sort of like a dream per se, and it may take anywhere from a few hours to a whole day. My goal today is to give you all the information you need, and then if you agree to proceed, we can schedule the procedure for another day. But first, what brings you here, young man?"

"What brings me here? Frankly, that's a good question I am still asking myself. I'm afraid the only answer is my friend's persistence."

In a scornful tone I continued, "Excuse me for my bluntness, Dr. Chapman, but what do you think you can actually do for me? I have visited a bunch of psychologists and psychiatrists before; strong medications and empty words never solve any real problems, and I am not convinced some mumbo-jumbo hypnosis will either. In fact, has this experimental method you do ever helped anyone? Let's first talk about that before talking about me."

I still feel ashamed for talking to such a respectable person in a tone like that. I can't offer any excuses, but only admit that I was not that same considerate and respectful Hadi I used to be. Love and kindness had given way to resentfulness and anger in my heart.

She said with a confident yet kind voice, "Yes, it has helped many, but in your case, I don't know yet. Perhaps it will help, perhaps not, but I wouldn't know for sure until I know what you are here for. Anyway, though, I assure you I'm here to sincerely try my best to help. If you trust me enough to just share your story, I promise to do my best, and who knows, maybe I could help."

In my head, that pessimistic voice was whispering, *she doesn't care about you! She only cares about the money she makes off of you. Can she turn the time back to before that horrible night? Of course not! She can't recover the amazing possibilities that are now lost! You tried three other therapists, Hadi; why would this one be any different? She is just another shrink! Empty words can't change anything in reality, you know that, don't you!?*

Although suppressed by trauma, the optimistic part of my mind was urging me to take any chance to recover my lost hope for true love. This part of my mind was whispering, *Hadi, you worked so hard all your life to find your one and only love! I know you are tired! I know you are hurt! And I know you have almost lost your faith in love, but true love is still real, independent of your experience and you know it deep in your heart, don't you? Let's give this a shot! You are here, after all, and so it doesn't hurt to just tell her about your pain, does it?*

For a few seconds, silence ruled the room as I was staring at the carpet on the floor, captured in the middle of this civil war between the pessimist and optimist in my head. Suddenly, I remembered something that my mom always reminded all her children: "If you try, you may fail or succeed. But if you don't try, it is guaranteed that you will fail!" So after all, I decided to open up to Dr. Chapman and genuinely give her method a chance.

Although I was still skeptical, I said in a tone that was humbler and less aggressive, "There is a lot to say, but for starters, my life is a love story with a sad ending. It's the story of a person who believed in the existence of a pure and true love and fought for it. It is the story of a person who believed his future love deserves the best and strived to improve in every aspect of life just to be worthy of that love. I know true love is real because I have always felt it, alive and strong right here in my heart. But now I have doubts that this kind of love ever existed outside my mind. I am not perfect, but I have always done everything in my life whole-heartedly so that I might live a life full of love! But here I am, broken and hopeless!" Tears started to find their way down my cheeks, cold tears mourning that lost love.

Dr. Chapman patiently waited while I got my act back together; then said, "Hmm. True love? That's brilliant! Tell me more."

"Yes, the empty dream of true love I guess, something I patiently strived for all my life, but in the end, all that has led me here! In comparison, I have seen many people with terrible intentions or personalities to be considered attractive and popular. You know, doctor? I really don't mean to generalize, but it seems like many people select their romantic partners based on superficial things like good looks, money, and empty romantic gestures rather than patiently searching for true love. It seems like, to many people, love is just a game where the winners are the first ones to find relationships that satisfy their own needs. It makes me think a lot of people have either forgotten what true love is, or they just like the idea of love but don't consider it realistic. It seems like the romantics like me, who want to take it slow and not quickly settle, are seen as losers in this society. It is extremely painful when I see after so much effort, I haven't found anyone who would put in the time to get to know me to discover the pure love I have to offer underneath this average appearance. Actually though, I knew one girl who had a deep understanding of true love in her beautiful heart, but..." That's when I lost it again and the baggage of memories broke into tears.

Obviously, I was dealing with dark feelings those days, feelings that only a severely broken heart can understand. I didn't mean to be too harsh on myself or too dramatic, but the games life play with us can bend every person's back at times.

Dr. Chapman said with a curious tone, "Interesting. Just one question though! Do you often speak this openly about love to everyone?"

I said, "Yes, I do if the conversation comes up. I think I know why you ask this question, though. You probably think that my openness about love may weird out a lot of people, don't you?"

She said, "Well, yes that might happen in some cases. I think you are already aware that talking this openly about love may make some people uncomfortable in Western culture, especially in one-on-one conversations. I am no expert on this topic, but in my experience, this culture is steeped in irony and many people look down on intense expression of emotions— especially in men. So, I wonder if your openness, although frank and honest, might have contributed to your failures in finding love. What do you think?"

I said, "I don't think that is the reason why I didn't find love. Initially, when I was new to this country, I had two unsuccessful first dates where I talked about my intentions of true love and I could see this unease on my dates' faces. I couldn't immediately understand how an honest conversation could make people so uneasy, but in order to adapt to these cultural differences, I soon changed my behavior. I also don't think I should censor myself on such an important topic, so there is a trade-off."

She continued with a warm and friendly smile, "Well done

then! That's great that you have the ability to learn from your experiences. Also, let me understand better, dear: Is your problem with the society in general or is it with a particular person?"

I said, "Both! But it's a long story! In short, I have a sacred light in my heart! I want to have true love but the majority of people care more about pleasures than true love. Also, I had a particular girl in mind, but I ruined everyone's life by being a coward! So I am just disappointed with everyone, including myself!"

She said, "Alright then, Mr. Shamsi! Although this conversation was shorter than other usual introductory appointments with patients, I think you'll find my treatment very helpful. I have been practicing this unique Jungian hypnotherapy that I developed for eight years now, so I am rather good at quickly sorting out who may not benefit from it. The method works particularly well when the source of distress is a series of contradictory yet profoundly deep feelings. As far as I can tell, you seem to feel a deep thirst for true love from one side, and a hodgepodge of exhaustion and anger from the other side. Your distress, Mr. Shamsi, will be alleviated only when these contradictory feelings somehow form a new constructive entity. Only when you achieve this balance will your life be restored from its ruins like a phoenix reborn from its ashes. Allow me to explain with an example that you might better relate to. You wrote in your medical file that you have a PhD in engineering, is that right?"

I said, "No, I don't have one yet, but I'm studying towards it."

She continued, "Brilliant! Are you familiar with how the industrial revolution started in the seventeenth century?"

I said, "Of course I am! Steam engine, isn't it?"

She continued, "True! As you know, back then engineers invented steam engine, which worked through a harmony between fire and water."

The nerd in me interrupted her, "Yeah, a steam engine

easily had the working power of at least tens of horses, if not hundreds, which was a huge deal back then! It revolutionized many industries and became the basis for today's scaled-up manufacturing systems. As an engineer, I have always admired those hard-working and genius early innovators!"

She said, "Exactly right! The point is they made water and fire work together in one place. Obviously, water and fire act against each other in nature, right? Water shuts off fire and fire could evaporate all the water away. But you know better than I that when these two elements of nature were put in a system to work together as part of a unified entity, it created huge power and potential! I can see how a similar process may be used in your mind. I believe there is a good chance my treatment method can find a way to teach your contradictory but deep feelings to work together and form a new constructive unity, a holy internal marriage per se!"

Despite my prejudice towards her profession, she was admittedly quite good at what she did! All of those shrinks I had seen over the past year treated me as if I was sick. Their understanding of me—and as such, their treatment—was always entrapped in the box of the presumption that something was wrong with me! Dr. Chapman, however, clearly stood out right in this first session. She never called me depressed or saw anything inherently wrong with me. Instead, she saw the potential of solving the internal dilemma I was dealing with through a very positive point of view. Her point of view wasn't that I was sick and needed to be cured; her point of view was that I was struggling with an internal conflict, and she wanted to find the source of that contradiction and turn it into a harmony.

Having been trained as a scientist, I often take the time to know the nitty-gritty of things, but the basic idea behind her treatment made so much sense that I was convinced she sure knew what she was doing. So I was already sold out on her suggested type of therapy, even if it was experimental. All the doubt I had at first towards her therapy was now gone! Poof!

I was still definitely unsure whether I get any good results out of this, but it seemed well worth the try.

So in response, I said in a tone that sounded like Archimedes' eureka moment, "Wow! That does make sense! It actually makes a lot of sense!"

She nodded her head in confirmation of my decision in a way that made her look very wise and said, "I'm glad it does, darling!"

Then, she stood up from her chair, walked towards the bookshelf, grabbed one of the handout notes, and handed it over to me; then said, "This handout describes, in detail, all you need to know about my therapy technique. In short, this technique is a combination of three psychological methods: hypnotism, Jungian analysis, and some eastern hermetic practices. You probably have heard of hypnotism, but Jungian analysis is the method in which psychologists try to understand the unconscious as the deep root of our mental state and this is commonly done through interpreting the dreams. However, I have discovered that it is a much more effective tool if practiced through a hypnotic trance. Let me not bore you with my fancy terms and expressions. You can find all the information and lots of links in this handout. In practice, I will put you under a hypnotic trance, and once that happens, it will feel like you are dreaming. You will see the sequence of memories, thoughts, actions, or anything that somehow had an impact on your current distress without consciously remembering that you are hypnotized or even that you are in my office. It will feel as if you are narrating your own story of life. You won't hear or see me, but I will be directing what event of your life you will see in these dreams. Like I said before, this technique has shown no side effects whatsoever in the past, but all the detailed information is in the handout."

She sat back in her chair and said, "I suggest you read all you need and research as much as you want and then you can call us to schedule a whole-day appointment if you want to proceed. Also, there is a consent page at the end of the handout that you need to sign and bring back with you to our office."

I said, "I don't think I need to read anything! I think I would like to give this a chance!"

She said, "Very well then, Mr. Shamsi. Talk to Nancy, the nurse who walked you to my office, and she will schedule you an appointment."

I took a look at the clock on the wall—it was almost 9 am already. My appointment was over, so I had to leave. I stood up and said, "Alright! It was good meeting you Dr. Chapman."

She said, "Oh, pleasure's mine! I'll look forward to seeing you again, Mr. Shamsi!"

I opened the door and, while holding the door handle, said, "By the way, you can call me, Hadi, if you want to."

She said with a smile, "Very well Hadi. Have a lovely day!"

I spoke with Nancy that same day, and scheduled a whole-day appointment for the next Friday.

On the way home, I was replaying the conversation we had in her office. The more I was thinking about it, the more promising her treatment sounded. She wanted to unify the internal conflict between my believing in true love on one hand and all of my painful experiences searching for love, on the other. That sounded amazing and I was hoping it could work, but how she planned to do this was still a mystery. I really had no idea what could come out of this treatment, or if it would be effective at all. So truth to be told, the pessimistic voice in my head visited me on multiple occasions after that day trying to convince me to cancel my next appointment with her, but this time, I was not giving in to that pessimistic voice.

A few days passed. On Thursday night before the next appointment, I was very relaxed and really looking forward to see how the treatment would go the day after. I went to bed early that night to prepare myself for the whole-day therapy. That night I had a dream, a very special one. It was a special dream for me because it was full of love.

Dr. Chapman had mentioned that Jungian analysts like her have expertise in interpreting dreams. So the next day, excited to discuss my dream with her, I got to Dr. Chapman's office very early in the morning even before Nancy, the nurse, showed up. I was excited about the whole thing. I wanted to share with her the excitement that dream had given me and how I was taking that dream as a good sign from the universe, a sign that maybe her method could help me rediscover the way. I desired true love so badly that even dreaming of it filled me with new life.

Anyway, the receptionist and the doctor eventually showed up and I was called for the treatment. When I got to her office room, Dr. Chapman was sitting on the same chair near the couch, drinking what I assumed to be tea. She said, "Good morning, Hadi! How are you today?"

Once again, I was impressed by the charming energy of the room. The first thing that caught my attention this time was the dream catchers she had hung from the ceiling. I had seen dream catchers for the first time only a year ago in a friend's house. Apparently, they are used by Native American tribes to repulse evil spirits that they believe cause bad dreams. In the background, a relaxing instrumental hymn was being played in a CD-player. The furniture was all very comfortably arranged around a nice wooden table on top of which there was a vase of beautiful and fresh flowers spreading a great smell in the room. I didn't notice this last time in her office, but she had placed a few incense sticks in an elephant-shaped crystal vase on the table. A nice ray of sunshine was entering through the window that day. I answered, "I'm doing great. Thank you! Did you know your office design catches my eye every time? I don't know what it is about it, but for some reason, it feels like home!"

She smiled and said, "Oh! Thank you, darling. That's very kind of you."

I said in a rushed voice, "By the way, Dr. Chapman. I had an interesting dream last night and I have so much to tell you! You said, as a Jungian analyst, you can interpret the dreams, right? "

Dr. Chapman answered, "Good heavens! I would love to hear your dream!"

I said, "In the dream, I was lying down on my side in a beautiful valley full of flowers and trees. Then all of a sudden I heard a voice, the same voice I had heard before in my previous dreams—the same angel-like feminine whisperer of love. The voice was calling my name over and over again, 'Hadi! Hadi!' Suddenly, the source of that feminine voice appeared in the shape of a magical light, floating and dancing around in the breeze. I got up and danced around with her. I followed her everywhere, but then after a point I could not go any further, as if there was a glass wall between us.

Then all of a sudden, she disappeared from the other side of the glass wall. In less than a second, I heard her whisper in my ear as if she was now standing right behind me. She said, 'My dearest Hadi, your love is like a diamond in the rough; don't give up on love and you will one day find me. I see the light of your diamond even if it has collected rust on the surface.' I tried to turn back to see her once again, but before I could do that, I woke up."

I continued, "Dr. Chapman! Maybe this is just a simple dream. I mean maybe I'm making a fool of myself by being so excited over just a dream, but I want true love so badly that even dreaming of it is so holy and sacred. Let the cynics of this world judge me, but love is my backbone and I'm proud of it."

Dr. Chapman said in a calming voice, "I know, young man! I know how you feel!"

She continued, "I will tell you the meaning of your dream later, but now let's get ready for the treatment, shall we?"

I said, "Sure!"

She lit two sticks of incense and asked me to get as comfortable as I could on the couch. She pulled a small wooden stool right in front of me and sat on it. Then, she started to recite words in a different language that I didn't recognize. She continued to do this for a couple of minutes; in all honesty, I was getting bored and tired. She then reached her hand towards me, and right when she did this, I felt an extreme urge to close my eyes. This was the last time I remembered her presence in the room until I woke up again in the same spot eight hours later.

It took only a blink of an eye! I closed my eyes to Dr. Chapman in front of me and immediately opened them to a different place. When I opened my eyes, there was nothing around; I was sitting on the same couch but surrounded with absolute darkness. My body felt light and my skin was shining. I had never experienced anything like that before! Even though I knew it was a dream, it looked as vivid as real life. It felt like I had been instantly teleported to a dark place outside of time and space.

As confused as I was, I thought to myself, *What the heck happened? How did she do that? Where am I?* I looked in every direction I could, up and down, left and right, I was surrounded by nothing but absolute darkness. I shouted, "Hello! Is there anyone out there?" then waited for a few seconds but no one responded. I continued calling out this time much louder, "Dr. Chapman?! Are you there?" but again no response but utter silence. Luckily, before I totally freaked out, the darkness in the surrounding space started to fade away. I found myself in my parents' home in Saudi Arabia. My parents were there. My siblings were there too. After a bit of confusion, I remembered I had seen all these scenes before in real life. I was actually walking into my own memories from the past. For some reason, I felt an urge to talk about them and narrate my own memories, and so I did:

CHAPTER TWO

I was born and raised in a poor neighborhood of Riyadh, called Al-Batha, in an immigrant family. Not too far from my home, you can find Al-Batha market. It's a noisy place with cars honking, vendors yelling, pedestrians fearlessly jaywalking in the midst of moving cars, and trash everywhere on the streets. You can find almost anything in this market: vegetables and fruits, spices, items of clothing, electronics, or even live chickens or seafood. It's quite cosmopolitan as you can find immigrants from many countries such as India, Malaysia, Afghanistan, Sudan, and others. Even though it's not the safest neighborhood nor the fanciest market in town, many of the lower-income immigrants go there because it's much more affordable compared to the malls where the wealthier locals shop.

Long before I was born, my parents had immigrated from the poor rural south of Iran to Saudi Arabia in the hope of finding stable jobs, but things hadn't worked out as planned. They often had to work in strenuous conditions for really low wages, and were often looked down upon by locals. Saudi Arabia is not generally known for its immigrant-friendly environment, especially not when you are from its historic rival, Iran.

As a child, I lived with my family in a tiny apartment we were renting, which was much nicer than the alternative—living in the filthy and poorly-maintained labor camps. Our apartment was comprised of two small rooms and a bathroom, and all six of us lived in this small home together. At night, one room was mom and dad's bedroom and the other room was both the kitchen and the bedroom for me and all of my siblings.

A lot of people in western countries think there is no sign of poverty in Saudi Arabia. Most westerners picture all Saudi Arabians as filthy-rich sheikhs fascinated with luxury cars and diamond-mounted watches! However, many people in that country, and especially migrant workers, deal with extreme poverty on a daily basis. The Saudi government is a family enterprise; that is, money, fame, and welfare are all in the hands of few families who are connected to the King's family. In fact, there are many lower-class families living in severe poverty with no rights whatsoever, and I was raised in one of those families.

My dad is an hourly-wage construction worker. He couldn't really spend much time with his family; he had to work two, or sometimes three, shifts to be able to feed us. Growing up, it was always heart-breaking to see my parents needing to work so hard even to the point of jeopardizing their health. It was very common for my dad to go to work at 4 am and come back no earlier than 10 pm, so by the time he made it home, he was usually exhausted and went straight to bed after a small dinner, making it hard for any of his children to actually see him every day, not to mention spending any quality time together.

My mom is the kindest angel on the planet. To outsiders, she looked like a typical Middle Eastern wife, but only her children knew the depth of sacrifices she made every day for her family. Not only did she act as a mom for four children, but also worked as a maid for a very rich Saudi family to help my dad with expenses. Realizing we did not have our dad around much, she tried her best to fill the empty place our dad left at home, too. She always had some time for her children and husband even though she worked non-stop inside and outside the home.

I also have one sister and two brothers. My sister and one of my brothers are both about ten years older than me. I have a younger brother too, who is two years younger. Of course, just like any other family, we sometimes fought and sometimes we were best friends.

If I was to use one color to describe how happy I was as a child, it would be gray. I was an energetic and healthy kid, so I am really thankful for that, yet life can be really hard when your parents work the entire time. And the worst part is that even though both my parents worked, we still lived in a constant state of poverty. Financial insecurity to us was an inextricable part of the family, like a sibling. Many nights we did not have proper food to eat, so my mom would soak the dried-up bread from past meals in water to make it edible. You can imagine how tough every other aspect of life was for us.

In the hypnotic dream I was, I had found my eight-year-old self in one of my memories in our home in Saudi Arabia. That night, my dad happened to be home a bit earlier from his second shift, so we all got to have dinner together. Following the Middle-Eastern dinner etiquette, we all sat on the ground around a piece of cloth and put the food in the middle. We had a big piece of Naan bread, a bit of cheese, and some herbs and vegetables for dinner, a rather cheap but tasty combination. During the dinner conversation, my dad broke the big news to us that my uncle's oldest son was getting married and he had invited all of us to go for his son's wedding to Iran, all costs paid by my uncle. I could see his eyes sparkling when he told us the news. Dad had come to Saudi more than fifteen years ago, but had not been able to go back and visit his own family since then. I was also super excited to meet my extended family, and especially looking forward to meeting my cousin, who was three years older than me. After what seemed like an eternity, the time of the wedding finally came and we flew there with tickets that uncle had bought us.

My uncle was a rich guy, very educated and accomplished, and so he had provided a life of comfort and luxury for his family. They lived in a big, fancy house decorated with artwork all over it, from marble statues to antique Persian paintings and rugs. As a kid, the contrast between their wealth and our poverty, although a feed to my curiosity, meant nothing much more. I was just excited to play with my cousin.

Everything was going awesome until I saw a personal computer in my cousin's room. I had never seen anything like that before. So being the curious kid I was, I asked my cousin in a very excited voice, "Wow! Do you have a TV for yourself in your room?"

He laughed and said, "No, you silly! It's a personal computer."

I answered, "A personal computer?! What is it used for?"

He said, "I play games on it, computer games."

I said, "I want one too. Is it expensive to buy one of these?"

My question about the cost was, of course, a naive but innocent conversation-opener, and I knew it was something my family probably could not afford. However, I can still remember the pain I felt when he answered, "Don't bother! It's too expensive for you anyway!" with a scornful giggle.

Some children have to face the tough realities of life much sooner than normal. My cousin's answer made me develop many grown-up questions in my head since an early age, like about the wealth inequality and the hunger that we sometimes felt through the core of our bones. Yet I was able to get past it in a very positive manner. I learned pretty quickly how to adapt. Growing up, I did not have cell phones, computers, or a lot of other things that other kids had, but I was sure about one thing even as a kid: none of those belongings were enough to bring human-beings a true happiness. Although not having enough money to cover the necessities of life is tough, having a ton of it won't make people happier than simply having enough.

After coming back from our trip, my understanding of our

financial situation and why my parents worked so hard had improved. Seeing the long hours my mom and dad had to work, one day, I brought up the idea that I could work while also attending school. I wanted to take some of the burden off their shoulders. My mom was entirely against this, but my dad could see in my eyes that I had the guts for it, so he persuaded her to agree. It was tough to both work and study at the same time for a kid who also needed to play, but it taught me how to strive for better.

Soon after, my mom found me my first part-time job. Like I mentioned before, she was a maid in the house of a wealthy family. The owner of the house was Sheikh Mohammed Faris. He was from a rich family that had very strong ties to the government of Saudi. It's hard to believe, but this guy had four formal and legal wives! In Saudi, "Sharia' law" based on the teachings of Wahhabi faith, allows a man to have up to five wives if he is rich enough to afford it. You can read between the lines about how terrible the human rights situation is in that country just by thinking about the polygamy laws! Anyway, Sheikh had bought a house for each one of his wives and was spending one week a month with each of them.

My mom had developed companionship with this guy's fourth and youngest wife over the years while working there as a maid. Sheikh's fourth wife was lonely three weeks of the month, and my mom had always gone above and beyond for her—not only as a maid, but as a friend. So when mom asked her to hire me, she didn't refuse. Sheikh's wife offered me a job as a part-time gardener for their yard.

Taking on the responsibility of a garden while not knowing much about gardening was a bit scary, but I could not have been more excited. To be able to work and contribute to my family gave me great satisfaction. Also, I had always loved plants and flowers, so this was a perfect job for me.

I had only one week to start the job and had to somehow educate myself about gardening. As a natural nerd with limited means, I spent many hours researching in the library where I could access countless gardening books for free. I took buses for one hour each way every day to get to a public library and started reading heavily. The result was great. After just one week, I had educated myself on the basic tools and practices of gardening.

Although Sheikh Faris had five sons from his other wives, he had only one child from his fourth wife: his only daughter, Lila. Lila is a pretty common name in Arabic for girls and it means night. My mom had heard from her mother that she named her Lila because she was born on a beautiful night. At the time I started working at their house, little Lila was only seven years old, one year younger than me.

When Sheikh was in the house, he would never let Lila to come to the yard. Sheikh was a very conservative Wahhabi Muslim, and he believed it was best for everyone if women were kept separated from men at all times. However, three weeks out of the month, Sheikh lived with his other wives in different houses, so Lila was able to sneak out to the garden.

The garden was full of roses, jasmine, and sun flowers. I have had a few different jobs in my life, but that gardening experience was the most amazing one.

The first time I met the seven-year-old Lila was one of those days when she came to the garden to play. It was the middle of December and the weather was heavenly: not too cold, not too hot. Riyadh is usually very hot, but around November till February, the weather could feel nice enough for the flowers to bloom. For some flowers in the garden, December is the best time of the year to prune them. So one afternoon, I was pruning the flowers in the corridor when I felt a tiny hand gently tapping on my back. I turned around to find a plump little girl with dark hair and beautiful eyes.

"What are you doing?" she said in a cute voice.

I explained to her that I was pruning some of the flowers and that pruning is needed to make some plants grow healthily and beautifully. I remember she asked tons of questions, one after another. You know, the kind of random questions kids ask at that age; I tried to answer all of her questions with patience.

This wasn't the first and last time. After that day, when I was doing my job in the garden, she would frequently come out to the garden. We talked, played, and laughed together, and gradually became friends.

At least in the beginning, it was not very easy for me to both work and study at the same time, but from the time I developed a friendship with Lila, this job had found another meaning. Just to be around her, I was often spending more time in the garden than I was paid for. She had no siblings, so she valued our time together too. I could see a charming light of joy in her eyes every time we played.

I heard from my mom that her mother was also happy about our friendship. Before Lila and I became friends, her mother had been concerned about Lila being lonely. However, we kept this friendship a secret from her dad because of his conservative Wahhabi beliefs.

Everyone one of us could get into deep trouble if Sheikh knew about this simple friendship between a boy and his daughter. In Wahhabi faith, any interaction between an unrelated male and female must be avoided if at all possible. Wahhabi belief sees any type of love before marriage as an act of the devil, impure and troubling. I am no expert in any religion, but in my opinion, Wahhabi belief attaches a high degree of sexual connotation to even the simplest relationships between an unrelated man and woman. This is why it forces women to cover themselves in the most unappealing outfit from head to toe. This may also be why they do not tolerate any romantic feelings between man and woman before marriage. As for me, I obeyed the rules as much as necessary in order to avoid getting myself into trouble, but not out of any personal conviction. Even though I respected other people's beliefs, I could personally never understand why anyone would follow such close-minded view of life.

Over time, my friendship with Lila was developing on deeper levels. For example, I remember one day she came home from her elementary school and she was sad. When I asked what happened at school, she said some bullies in her class called her fat. I told her, "Lila, you are a very beautiful girl! Don't let anyone tell you otherwise."

Of course, as a kid, she wasn't convinced by what I said, but later I heard the bullying problem was resolved through her dad's intervention in the school board.

Lila and I kept our friendship going for about five years. We were playmates until her dad asked me to work in his garage. He had multiple high-end luxury cars in his personal garage, and wanted someone trustworthy to keep them in shape, clean, and ready for his sons' nightlife rallies in the streets. The garage was located in Sheikh Faris' main house, the one that his first wife and three of his sons lived in and not the one Lila and her mom lived in. Of course, it was very difficult for me to let go of my gardening job, which meant not seeing Lila, perhaps ever again. But I didn't have a choice. My options were to either accept the new job or, most likely, not have a job anymore. Perhaps, Sheikh had sensed that both Lila and I were growing up and he didn't want to risk having a teenage guy near his only daughter. Anyway, I took this new job when I was thirteen.

Being from a poor family, my parents always put huge pressure on us to be the best in our schools in the hope that someday we achieve high levels of education and get better jobs than they could get. In the eyes of my parents, education was the only way a poor person could work their way up to a reasonable job and a decent salary. My mom wanted me to be either a medical doctor or an engineer, and my dad wanted me to be either an engineer or a lawyer. I had been studying really hard while working, which left me no time to spend on anything else.

My teenage years were passing quickly with me focusing on my school. I had to work and study hard at the same time. One of Sheikh's sons was a teenager too. His life and mine, of course, weren't at all comparable. He used his sweet teenage years to enjoy life, but I used them to be able to feed myself, help my parents, and try to make a better life for my future family. Don't get me wrong—I wanted to have a level of comfort and welfare to enjoy my life too, but given the circumstances I was living in, I chose to do the right thing rather than what I desired. This internal fight against selfishness was something I practiced from a young age, which led me to who I am now.

Four years passed and I was still working part time in Sheikh's garage. Sometimes, my mom would tell stories of her work at home and occasionally, Lila's name would come up in the conversations, but that was it. I never dared to ask specifically about Lila. I was shy and at the same time, did not want to give my family the impression that I was missing Sheikh's daughter.

For many of us, teenage years are a critical time of our lives when many things change, including our physical appearance, our voices, and even our mentalities. I was going through the same period of my life back then. I was not an aggressive teenager in general, but in all honesty, all those hormonal changes I was going through led to few episodes of teenage rebellion. I remember picking a physical fight with a bus driver who incorrectly accused me of free riding.

My teenage years felt as uncomfortable as a caterpillar might feel developing in a tiny cocoon and hoping to eventually transform into a butterfly. Or, maybe a butterfly developing into a caterpillar in my case. My nose seemed to get bigger every day, my face was showing pimples, and my voice was getting thicker. Apart from all the physical changes I was experiencing in my body, those days were challenging times of trying to reshape my identity as a soon-to-be-adult. I was struggling with finding my own meaning in life in the confusing and challenging teenage years. I had not yet figured what makes me happy in life until a certain dream shaped the path of my life forever. This wasn't an ordinary dream, but one that I'd like to consider divine. This dream enabled me to clearly see my way to ultimate happiness. After that dream, I was not the same person. After that dream, I knew exactly what I wanted in life.

I remember clearly that it was the beginning of summer.

That night I was sleeping in the main room with my two brothers since our sister had already got married and was not living with us anymore. Near the dawn, I had this strange dream:

I saw myself walking in a river. I could feel the pleasure of walking in a very clear water of that river, so clear that I could see those round and smooth stones at the bottom of the river. I took a look at my surroundings. On my right-hand side, the sun was shining in the sky; the land was filled with beautiful flowers and trees. On my left, there was a crescent moon with stars in the dark sky of the night and what appeared to be bushels of grass. I kept walking in that shallow river towards the horizon.

All of a sudden, I heard a very clear voice in the sky that called my name, "Hadi, be strong!"

I focused my attention on the source of the river on the horizon. I saw an angel-like feminine figure appearing on the horizon. Her eyes shined like stars, her body covered with a cloth of silk, and her hair floating in the air in all the directions.

I don't know why I came up with this question in the dream, but I asked, "Tell me, angel: what is the most precious in life?"

The angel-like figure answered with her heavenly voice, "Deep in your soul, you know the answer, don't you? Be neither fearful nor sad, for you have the gift of pure love!"

I abruptly woke up! That was a shocking dream, the first of many! It felt so real it took me a while to realize I was dreaming. To my surprise, for a couple of seconds after opening my eyes, I could still hear the sound of the streaming river underneath my feet. I did not talk with anyone at home about that dream; I just put on my clothes and immediately left the house. I walked out in the streets for an hour, thinking this dream might be the answer to all of my questions about true happiness. Now, I could truly feel with every bone in my body that true love was my purpose, the ultimate goal of everything in my life. I always pursued money, better career, better life, but all of that was done to make myself more deserving of that one and only love I would meet in the future.

I had found my ultimate goal. My life had found a meaning that I could truly feel in the very depth of my heart. Nothing in life could be stronger. After that dream, I decided to devote my life to my love. I did not know exactly who my love was going to be, but that didn't matter; I just wanted to deserve her sacred presence. I wanted to be a good man for her from every aspect! I wanted to be able to make her happy. She meant everything to me, literally; so much that without her, nothing else had any meaning. My life had a goal and a plan now.

Back in the day, the government of Saudi offered few financial scholarships to some exceptional third and fourth-grade high school students. This spectacular scholarship provided qualified students with full tuition for the best academic institutes of Saudi Arabia and a stipend throughout their four-year study in college. This was a great opportunity for under-privileged kids like me, but as you can imagine, it was very competitive too. Before the dream, I was not very hopeful I would get in. I was studying well, but since I had not figured out what exactly I wanted to do in life or what my ultimate goal was, I was not yet determined nor focused enough for such competitive program.

But after this dream, I decided to triple up on studying hard to get the scholarship. The scholarship was my gateway to providing a good life for my future family, and now, I was more determined than ever. I aspired to make it to the top hundred students in the country in order to get the government full-bright scholarship. After that dream, my ambition got a boost. Love made me refuse to accept failure; I imagined nothing but success.

I was seventeen and I had one year until the big nation-wide exam for the scholarship. There was nothing that could stop me; neither tiredness, nor lack of sleep, nothing. Love had already made me a more determined person. Love gave me the courage to work extremely hard and stay at the top of my game. All I had was my dream of true love, and what a wonderful motivation that was!

It was at the peak of my preparatory studies that my dad lost his both jobs. I remembered him coming home one day at around 4 pm, which was pretty unusual. He went straight to the corner of the room and sat there holding his knees and head with his hands. This was typical body language for my dad when he was disappointed or sad, so everyone quickly realized something bad had happened. He then told us that his boss had replaced him with some other workers who were less experienced and cheaper in order to cut costs.

He soon started looking for a new job, but we all knew that it could take a while. We had always been living paycheck to paycheck, so my dad losing his jobs meant a lot of financial pressure on us. I had previously planned to quit my job at Sheikh's garage to focus on studying, but now with my dad losing his jobs, I could not be selfish and do that. My family needed the money I was bringing home from that part-time job, at least until my dad found another job. That meant I had to work hard to keep the job and study well to win the competition.

Many other students who were competing had a lot of private lessons. Their families provided them with a quiet and relaxing environment, but in my case, all I had was my determination and the books from the public library. My family could never afford to pay for any extra classes; we could barely afford to feed ourselves properly in those days.

I was studying all the time—not much personal time for myself, normally getting only four or five hours of sleep for the last one year. It was not easy at all, especially under all the stress my family was going through! But all those hardships were sweet and fulfilling when I reminded myself that all of those sacrifices were for love.

Through studying for that exam, I came across an American short story in our literature course. The story was called "The Gift of the Magi," written by O. Henry in 1905. That story refined my initial idea of what true love is and gave me a role model for how I wanted to treat my one and only love. The story is about a very poor couple who are observing

Christmas and want to surprise each other with gifts. The husband owns a pocket watch but not much extra money. He sells the watch and buys a comb for his wife who has really beautiful long hair. They meet each other at home in the evening. The man is shocked to see that his wife has cut off all of her hair! He gives her the comb, which he bought with the money he made by selling his pocket watch, and she gives him a watch chain, which she had bought by selling her hair. Indeed, the man sold his best asset, his pocket watch, to give his wife a worthy gift, and his wife did the same for him. At the end of the day, the actual gift did not matter, but it was the selfless intention behind those gifts that was a testimony to their true love. They whole-heartedly and selflessly offered the best of themselves to each other.

So after a year of preparation, the day of the exam finally arrived. My assigned testing location was at a big school in a rich neighborhood, and I only had money to buy bus tickets to get there. I had to change three buses to get to that school with a little bit of walking, but I finally made it only ten minutes late. Don't get me wrong—I don't like to be late, especially for such important exam! I planned ahead and I woke up as early as the bus system started working. I got the first bus at 5 am that day, yet the distance was so far and the unpredictable bus was the only option a poor boy like me had. Anyway, I was late, but when I sat at my bench and received the question booklet, I took a deep breath and only reminded myself of my paramount motivation. That one last reminder that all of my efforts were for love gave me the most unimaginable focus on the test, and guess what? I nailed it! Among more than a million students who contested throughout the entire country, I earned the fifteenth rank, more than enough to be granted the full-scholarship.

Of course, my acceptance was not only great news to me, but it also brought my family extreme joy, so much so that they almost forgot all the financial problems they were dealing with. My mom cooked my favorite food that night and my dad hugged me so tightly when he heard the news and as tears were soaking in his eyes, he said, "You made me not worry about your future anymore; this is the best gift a son could give his dad."

About a month after the results of the test were announced, the registration process started. This prestigious scholarship gave me the choice to select any school in Saudi Arabia, and because of my interest in chemistry, I chose to study chemical engineering at one of the best schools in the country, King Saud University.

Until that time, I was working in Sheikh Faris' garage. Apparently his wife had told him about my accomplishment, which had made Sheikh very impressed. One day when I was working in the garage, I was told by my supervisor that Sheikh wanted to see me tomorrow after work in his fourth wife's house; that is, Lila's house where I used to be a gardener.

Meeting Sheikh was a big deal, and I needed to dress formally but I had no suit of my own. So the next day I wore my dad's old and off-fashioned suit. This was the suit he had bought for his own wedding when he was my age and it so happened that the suit fit me well. Anyway, I showed up and was permitted inside the building of the house. I had never seen the inside of Sheikh's house before. The house could define the word luxurious. Huge chandeliers, very beautiful carpets made up of silk, beautiful high-end furniture, walls decorated with little pieces of mirror making spectacular reflections. But I was thinking more about whether or not I would see Lila by accident. I mean, if only we ran into each other by chance—gosh, I had missed her so much…but this was a secret. No one could know!

I had seen Sheikh a few times before on random occasions like when he was visiting his cars in the garage, but I had never talked to him. After about ten minutes that I was sitting by his personal office room on second floor, the door opened and he came out of the room, looked at me and said, "Are you Hadi?" I said, "Yes, I am." Sheikh seemed a lot older and more broken down than the last time I had seen him. His hair and beard had turned white and he had lost considerable weight.

After the hand shaking and usual greetings, he invited me inside his office and while gesturing with his hand for me to sit down, he said, "I've heard that you received the government's full bright scholarship. I know only a few people among the millions of contestants receive that award! So well done, boy! Allah bless you!

I said, "Thank you, sir. I am very glad my hard work finally paid off."

Sheikh said, "You have been working in my house for about ten years now, right?"

I answered, "Yes, since I was eight years old, and now I'm eighteen."

He said in a pondering voice, "Masha-Allah!" He paused, leaned forward and continued, "Do you remember about three months ago one late night shift, you found a big stack of cash on the driver's seat when cleaning my car?"

I said with a slightly worried yet confident voice, "Yes sir, I do. And I submitted it to the garage supervisor without a penny less than I found."

He said, "Yes you did, but what you didn't know was that stack of cash was not just placed there because I had forgotten it. It was purposefully placed there because I wanted to test your trustworthiness. I have been watching your behavior for a while now."

He took a cigarette out of his pocket pack, patiently lit it with a match, and then continued, "I knew you and your family really needed money and that stack of cash could solve many of your problems. So I asked the supervisor to put it in my car when no one else except you were in the garage. I wanted to see if you'd take what isn't yours when you thought no one was watching."

He coughed a few times after taking the first puff of the smoke, and then pointed towards the side table near my seat and said, "Bring me that ash tray, will you?"

I took the ash tray and put it near his table.

He continued, "You see? Lila, my daughter, has registered for a great college preparatory school, but the school is far from here, and the problem is she, as a woman, is not allowed to drive. I would drive her myself, but I am seventy-one years old now and I don't physically feel as strong as when I was younger. May Allah bless my sons, but each is traveling back and forth to one side of the world, Europe, America, Thailand, and so on. So, my only choice is to find someone who has a history of serving our family, someone trustworthy. I can see you are a qualified boy and my wife seems to know your mom and family very well too, so I want to give you a job that requires a lot of trust. I want to assign you to be a chauffeur for Lila and her mom. It will pay a lot more than your current job and it will be a big help to your family too, and you all deserve it. So what do you say?"

I said in shocked and happy tone, "Absolutely, Sir! Thank you for trusting me."

He tapped his half-burnt cigarette over the ash-tray a few times and said, "Very well; thank Allah. I'm glad you accepted but remember very carefully: Lila is my only daughter and I love her very much. If I had any other choice, I would not offer this to a guy; but since there is no way around it, I selected someone like you who I can trust. You should remember all the time that I have my eyes on you and above all, Allah is watching. So be very cautious of your actions around my daughter. You must protect her at all times and at any cost as if she is part of your own honor. I will crush anyone who looks at my daughter with one dirty look. Do you fully understand the gravity of the situation?"

I said in a confident voice, "Yes sir, I do!" But even though I responded confidently, I was not so confident in my heart. I knew I liked Lila and I missed her, so I doubted I could be as neutral as Sheikh was asking me to be.

Finally, after some more small talk, I left the house.

This was unbelievable! I was going to see Lila again after so many years. It was as if a dream was coming true.

On the way out, I was debating my feelings for Lila in my head. By that time, I knew that the most important thing in my life was true love. I also knew that I really missed Lila, but I was still not sure if what I felt for her was love or not. I had more questions than answers: *Were those feelings really love? Was it possible that what I felt as love was only yet another hormonal change I was facing as a teenager? Was she the person who was meant to be my one and only love? How could I be sure that I wouldn't feel the same way towards another person? What was love, anyway?*

CHAPTER THREE

Soon after I started college, I started my part-time job as Lila's personal chauffeur too. In the archaic culture of Saudi Arabia, it was a huge deal that Sheikh trusted me to drive his daughter to and from school. I guess he seemed impressed with my scientific achievements and integrity. But I'm sure it was also because my mom was good friend of Lila's mom, and perhaps her mom's trust in my mom was the most essential but unspoken part of this equation.

My job was to take Lila to her school in the mornings, bring her back from the school whenever she was done, run personal errands for Lila and her mom, and be available to them whenever needed. The job was not hugely demanding, but required a significant amount of time management: The schedule for my classes had to fit the somewhat haphazard transportation needs that Lila and her mom had. For instance, I never took classes that were offered in the evenings because that was one of the popular times for her mom's shopping adventures. On the first day of the job, I received the keys for a brand-new 2005 white Mercedes with absolutely luxurious all-leather interior.

I showed up to her house the next morning, waiting for her. I was wearing the black suit and tie that were provided to me as working attire. My heart was coming out of my chest, beating like it had never beaten before. After a few minutes that felt like an hour, Lila opened the main door of the house, and walked down from the stairs. I held the back-seat door open for her and she got in the car as gracefully as a queen getting into the royal carriage. I started the car, and we headed towards her school.

Silently, the joy of seeing Lila again had filled my heart. She was definitely not that little girl I once knew. As a teenage girl in an extremely conservative country, she had to appear in Abaya every time she was out of the home. Abaya is a full-body Islamic dress that is almost forced upon women throughout Saudi Arabia. It covers every part of a woman's body except the face. However, some women wear another piece that covers the lower part of their face, leaving only their eyes and eyebrows out. In other words, it's a style that even the worst fashion designer on their worst day would never come up with! In the hot days of the summer, it is a disaster to deal with Abaya; a disaster that the women of Saudi Arabia are forced to deal with every day.

The distance from her home to the school could take us about half an hour—even more if traffic was heavier than usual. The first time she was in the car, absolute silence persisted for the first twenty minutes or so. She seemed to be too shy or too conservative to start the conversation. Also, I was paying a lot of attention to my driving, because my entire family's income in a year could not pay for the repair of one scratch on this fancy car. Finally, after we got really close to her school, I broke the ice by saying, "Excuse me, is the AC making it cool enough for you or should I turn it up a notch?"

She said, "No, its fine."

I continued, "By the way, I used to be a gardener in your house for many years. We used to play and laugh as friends when we were kids. Do you remember any of that?"

She answered in a shy voice, "Yes Hadi, I do. I remember everything. All the silly questions I used to ask you about flowers, nature, and basically any random thing in the world, and you patiently answering all of them. Gosh, I'm so embarrassed now for all those silly questions whenever I think about them."

To me, many of those questions were part of her charming curiosity. I laughed out loud, and said, "Don't mention it at all! It was all fun!"

Moments after this brief conversation, we arrived at her school, so I said, "Here we are. I will be waiting for you right here at 2 pm, but I'll stay as long as needed, so no rush!" I then jumped out of the car and opened the door for her.

Our first conversation after so many years was not very long, but I was thrilled to talk to her again. We had plenty of time to go over so many of those sweet memories we had from the time we were kids. I didn't know about her, but I remembered our time together as if it was yesterday—but I had to be careful. I really did like her, so if I allowed my emotions to rule my behavior, I would probably scare her off. I had many precautions and considerations in my head and was extremely careful to not reveal any interest in her.

In my college life that had started at the same time as my new job, things were going well. In fact, my efforts were continuously paying off. The first semester I gained second place among all students of the university from all levels, and this trend continued more or less. Many other full-scholarship recipients who had worked very intensely before getting into the program were just taking it easy in college. But I was motivated to provide the best life possible for my future love, so I worked to improve and to become the best of my class in college as well. Of course, it was not easy working and studying at the same time and doing both well, but I did it because I was determined to provide a better future for the love I had not yet met. True love had enabled me to fight against laziness, impatience, and selfishness.

One day, to broaden our somewhat limited topics of conversation, and also out of curiosity, I asked Lila what her field of study was in high school. Those days in Saudi's high schools, there were only a few major fields. After choosing a field in freshman year, students pretty much stuck with this field for their entire high school career, and perhaps even through college. These fields were human sciences, mathematics and engineering, natural sciences, and art. These four covered pretty much every educational path.

She told me that she was studying in the field of human sciences. Her dream was to study literature and poetry in college, and human science was the field to choose if you were interested in that.

This was the beginning of a series of conversations we had; a series of conversations about many different intellectual subjects. Sometimes, for example, I would start these conversations by asking about how she was doing in school and what they were learning. Many students, of course, could not care less about the courses in high school, but Lila was always very enthusiastic about all the subjects that they were studying. They had to write articles about many different subjects, from religion and philosophy to poetry and literature, but of course, all of these courses were structured according to very fundamental Wahhabi principles.

One hot day, she asked me to stop by an ice cream shop on the way back to her house, and so I did. I purchased two ice cream cones and brought them back to the car, but we rolled down the windows to enjoy it better. The ice cream shop was close to a bus station where my mom often changed routes. I don't know how low the odds are, but it so happened that right when we were at the ice cream shop that day, my mom was at the bus station across the street. She saw us and I saw her, but I don't think Lila paid attention. Mom did not approach us, but from the look of her face, I could tell that she was not happy about Lila and I having ice cream together.

That distinct look on my mom's face was clearly a sign that I was going to be in trouble when I got home. And I was right about that! Immediately after I got home, she asked my siblings to go to the other room and give us privacy. Then, she quickly approached me and asked in an angry voice, "Was that Sheikh's daughter you were having ice cream with today?!"

I said, "Yes, but—" Before I could finish my sentence, she suddenly slapped me hard across the face.

Bitter silence ruled between us for a long-lasting few seconds, staring at each other's eyes. I was definitely seeing anger in her eyes that gradually gave way to the tears brimming there. As she started crying out loud, she leaned towards the wall and squatted in the corner. I was in shock. I did not know what I had done to deserve this slap but at the same time, I was feeling sympathy for my mom. That poor woman had sacrificed a lot over years to raise four children in a financially deprived family, and I wouldn't blame her for losing her temper.

I gradually approached her, gently hugged her, and then whispered with a calming voice, "Mom, what's wrong?"

She kept on crying and said nothing in answer. I just let her cry for few minutes. I thought it was good for her to purge all the emotions and difficulties she had been bottling up.

After she stopped crying, she said, "Hadi, you can't jeopardize your family's future like that. You know what happens if Sheikh hears that you are flirting with his daughter?"

I became a bit defensive since I did not want to openly confess I really liked Lila. I knew that only would create more drama with my mom. I said, "Flirting?! Mom, she asked me to stop by to get ice cream and as a chauffeur, it is my job to do that. It's that simple!"

She stared into my eyes and asked, "Hadi, I'm your mom! I can tell from the glimmer in your eyes that you like her. Look straight into my eyes and tell me you don't like her. Go ahead, look!"

I looked into her eyes, but I couldn't hide the truth anymore. I said nothing and dropped my gaze to the floor.

When I broke eye contact with her, she said, "There it is! I knew it." She put her hands on her head as a sign of frustration and continued, "Hadi, this must not happen again! You know we desperately need our jobs to afford to raise you all. Not only that, but don't you know what happens if an influential man like Sheikh commits to taking revenge on you for talking to her daughter? Don't you know that in this country, he can probably send you to jail for even talking to a girl in public?!

Hadi, if you love your mom, please don't continue this. Promise me, okay?"

I said, "Mom...well, yes maybe I like her, but this goes back to when I was a child. I have never, even for a second, dared to look at her in an impure way."

Mom interrupted me, "That doesn't matter! Others don't know how pure your intentions are; they see only your actions and then judge you based on their own perceptions. Hadi, a rich man like Sheikh will never let a poor boy marry his only daughter, so just get it out of your system. Will you? This love is going to make trouble for you and your entire family. Promise me right now that you will get it out of your head!"

Mom rarely ever put me on spot like that, so when she did, I knew she wanted a definitive answer. However, what she was asking of me was unthinkable, so I said, "Mom, I have never wanted to create problems for others, especially not my own family. I'm sure you know that about me, but what you are asking is almost impossible. I can't just undo my life, my childhood memories with her, and my interest in her simply because you are asking me to. If anything good has happened in my life, true love has been the drive behind it. I have lived my entire life so far that way. I can't undo it."

Mom said in a begging voice, "But my dear..."

This time I interrupted her to finish my thought, "But I also understand the gravity of the situation very well. I cannot promise to change my feelings, but I can be more cautious not to show signs of them to her or anyone else. If I act formally all the time, no one will know what is in my heart. That's the best I can do, mom! But it really sucks to live in such a close-minded country that you have to fear for your life and freedom just for showing the subtlest signs of love. This country sucks with all its sheikhs and clerics!"

I said that and I left the house to end that conversation, at least for that night.

After that night, I tried to stand by my word and did everything I could to act like I was only a chauffeur and nothing more, but it wasn't always easy. If Lila asked for ice cream, I only bought it for her and made up excuses for myself. If she was shopping in the mall and needed me to follow her or carry her bags, I would walk with few feet of distance between us. For a while, I even tried to minimize conversations in the car and only answer what she asked.

After some time, though, I let our conversations in the car continue. I thought they were just harmless conversations and no one could see us talking, so there was no need to be fearful of any repercussions. Also, I think both she and I enjoyed these intellectual conversations during which we got to know each other better by revealing our similarities and differences.

I spent three years as one of the top students in the university as well as working as a chauffeur. Time had changed many things about us both. It wasn't only that we both had grown up in the years we spent apart. I soon realized that her mentality had changed too. Having been raised in a very conservative family, she followed and believed in most of the same extreme and fundamental beliefs of her father: The Wahhabi faith!

Wahhabi faith was founded about a hundred years ago by a guy named Abdul-Wahhab, who was famous for the most conservative and most aggressive interpretation of Islam. It is rumored that he and the governing family had an agreement that as long as the Saudi government enforced and supported Wahhabi faith, Wahhabi faith would also support the Saudi government in return—a mutually beneficial yet evil relationship. As a result, in Saudi's power pyramid, the closer you get to the top—the Saudi family—the more vigorously you must follow the Wahhabi faith, at least on the surface. Since Sheikh Faris was from a family with strong bonds to the government, of course, he brought up his children under extreme Wahhabi teachings and practices. As for Lila, our conversations showed that she clearly had an inner passion for her god, but also was quite intellectual about her beliefs. She firmly believed in and obeyed most of the Wahhabi rules, but at the same time, was not fearful to think independently and even question some of the practices.

I clearly remember the first time we ended up discussing our perspectives of love in an indirect way. It was a warm day around 2:00 in the afternoon and her college classes were over.

As usual, she sat in the back of the car as we drove towards her home. Her face looked excited and amazed. I thought she might be hungry after a long day, so I offered her a Snickers chocolate bar that she really liked, and asked, "So how were your classes today, Lila? Anything fun?"

She answered enthusiastically, "It was such a great day! Our literature teacher asked me to stay after class, and then she told me a few things that really made my day. She told me she appreciates that I show so much interest in literature and she sees so much talent and potential in me. We had a nice conversation about my passion for literature. My teacher actually gave me a book from a Persian poet called Hafiz, whose poems are about love. I read just a little bit, but I'm really fascinated by it. I think I have found a new passion in literature: Persian poetry! I am so excited that my teacher introduced me to it!"

"Oh wow! That's interesting; I'm so glad for you. By the way, did you know my parents were actually born in Iran, which technically means I am originally Persian? My dad immigrated here before I was born. Did you know that?" I said excitedly.

"Wow, thank Allah! So your parents should know about Persian culture, right? You probably can help me learn more about this beautiful poetry, then!"

"Absolutely! My mom has told me a lot about Hafiz and his love poems, and I can surely try my best to help you. Ask any time!"

She said, "That's great, Hadi! One thing I see over and over again is Hafiz's reference to wine, but he talks about a divine wine. I really don't understand. How can wine be divine?"

"Oh, that's a euphemism." I answered, "As you know, not too many years ago, the entire Middle East was ruled by kings who were sort of in bed with the Islamic clerics of the time, much like the situation in today's Saudi Arabia. To these rigid clerics, directly speaking of love was seen as earthly and sinful, as it was considered a distraction from Allah, and therefore forbidden and sometimes punishable. As a way to get around this, Persian poets found clever euphemisms that concealed their true meanings from the close-minded clerics. In this way, they could express controversial topics and ideas, and yet still be on the safe side."

Lila loved these euphemisms and was fascinated by the artistic expressions these poems had used to express love. I could see a light in her eyes that made them seem full of life when she was talking about these subjects. I continued, "Of course as you know, wine is forbidden in Islamic culture, but by introducing the euphemism of divine wine, they were really referring to true love. In their poems, they pretended they only meant love for Allah to avoid the prosecution of the rigid clerics. After all, when you think about it, love and wine have many things in common. You can lose yourself to both of them; both love and wine are best when aged; and both are result of a transformation, one biological and the other spiritual. Does that make sense?"

"Yes, it makes a lot of sense. That's fantastic!" she said and then opened the book of poems she had with her and started reading nonstop.

Our conversations about Persian poetry continued for some time and gradually led us to discuss our beliefs about love. I was particularly interested in learning that about her, but I knew this would most certainly be crossing the lines drawn by both my mom and Sheikh, yet I wanted to know her in a deeper way. I wanted to know if she shared the same convictions about love as I did, and so I allowed myself to cross those lines just for once.

One day in the car, in the middle of our conversation about poetry, I asked her, "So, Ms. Lila, we have been talking about the divine wine for a while. I know my heart has always been thirsty for that kind of wine, but how about you? I'm curious: have you ever wanted to experience that divine feeling too?"

I could see her cheeks blushing. After a few moments of

pause, she said, "That's what I have always dreamed of, all my life."

I said, "But aren't you afraid of the clerics of our time?"

She responded, "I am, but I believe in the word of Allah and not what the clerics want us to believe. I believe in my Abaya, in praying, in fasting, but not in the old-fashioned arranged marriage. You know how I question everything and there is no doubt in my mind that Allah wants us to fall in love, even though the clerics tell us we shouldn't."

This was a breakthrough moment in my life. It was at this moment that I found out Lila sought the same sacred true love I was seeking. It was also at this moment in my life that I finally fell in love with her. All the doubts I had in the past as to whether or not she was that true love I was looking for finally were gone. However, I still did not have the courage to do anything about it, so I kept my feelings towards her to myself until that day when destiny forced me to make a decision.

It was an early morning in the beginning of October. As part of the routine, I brought the car by the stairs of Lila's house and kept the AC running to make it nice and cool for her. She often seemed full of joy, but that day, she was different. She just simply walked down the stairs and got into the car, keeping her eyes fixed on the ground the whole time, without saying a single word. She seemed sad or angry.

During the ride, I waited to see if she wanted to start the conversation or not, but she was as silent as a rock. I wanted to know if this was just one of those days teenage girls at that age go through or if something serious had happened. And above all, I wanted to help. After a good amount of time, I dared to start the conversation. I asked, "Ms. Lila, how are you doing today? Is everything okay?"

I heard no response.

After a pause, I asked again in the hope of distracting her from the negative thoughts she seemed to be having, "It's Monday today! You have the literature class that you always enjoy. So what subject is your teacher going to cover today?"

Then, to my surprise, I heard her sobbing.

"What is it, Lila?" I said in an anxious tone.

As she was wiping the tears off her face, she explained to me what had happened the night before. She told me her dad had told her that she must marry the son of one of his influential friends. In other words, her dad had promised her to his friend's son a long time ago, according to the tradition of arranged marriage. The betrothal was a political move to join Sheikh Faris' tribe with the other influential tribe. According to Saudi traditions, if a girl's father promises her to anyone, she has no power to decline.

She explained that her husband-to-be was fifteen years older than her, and even worse, she had never met him. She explained that her dad had arranged for an official Islamic ceremony to be held in just three days.

The day had turned around for both of us and we were both in shock. Life had suddenly put both of us at a dangerous juncture. We both had the choice to either accept what life had put in front of us or make extremely radical decisions and accept the consequences. We both had only three days to choose our destiny.

I skipped all my classes that day and the two days that followed. I had a lot to process. Right after I dropped Lila off at her school, I returned the car to their house and then walked to a park near their house. I sat in a corner bench under the shade of a tree. It was a hot day, but my mind was so engaged that I did not really notice the temperature. I gave a lot of thought to the situation and it looked like I only had two options.

One option was to reveal my love for her and ask her dad to give me his blessing to marry her. Now, this choice could have two different results. If my feelings for Lila were mutual and I could somehow magically change her dad's mind, this option would be the right choice. But not only did I not know if Lila liked me or not, but it was also not really probable that a power-hungry man like Sheikh would allow Lila to marry a boy from such a poor family rather than a politically strategic match. The other scenario was if Lila's feelings for me were just those of a friend. This could lead to catastrophic consequences—not only for me, but also for my family. If Lila felt uncomfortable with me coming clean to her, then Sheikh would not only fire me and my mom, but also possibly send me to jail for advancing on a female. My family was really depending on the income from my mom and I to survive day by day. As I had promised my mom, I never wanted to jeopardize the life of my family, but at the same time, it was my love who was being forced to marry to someone else right in front of my eyes.

The other option was to not say anything and be silent forever, but how could I be silent and do nothing?! How could I let her marry someone she hadn't even met? When I knew her dream was to marry someone for love, how could I do nothing about her losing that dream? What kind of lover was I not to fight for her dream to come true? But on the other hand, I was asking myself, did she really need help from a poor chauffeur like me? After all, anything I could do might end up worsening the situation for her.

Two rough days and nights passed quickly. I was shocked, restless, confused, and uncertain. I had not slept or eaten much the past two days. There wasn't time. One more second spent on making the right decision could change both of our lives forever. Finally, I decided to listen to my heart and act like a lover. I decided to tell her how I felt about her in the hope that she would share the same feeling and if not, that she would keep it a secret.

That Wednesday late morning, I brought the car near the stairs, following the same routine. I was extremely anxious that day. This was supposed to be the first time ever that I confessed my love to any girl. I knew it was the day of destiny. Either we, together, could find a way out of this, or she had to be officially married to another man after the noon prayer. As usual, she sat in the car and I started driving, but this time, I was supposed to drive her to her dad's office where they had planned to do the official Islamic ceremony. I had only half an hour to reveal to her a love I had kept secret for years.

In order to make it less awkward for her, I had planned to only speak of love in the last ten minutes of the ride. We were both quiet for the first twenty minutes of the ride, but when it came to the time that I had to tell her how I truly felt about her, all of a sudden, it was as if my mouth had locked up. My heart started beating like crazy, my head was heavy—heck, I could not even breathe regularly. I was imagining my mom and siblings and what would happen to them if things went wrong.

We got there and she left the car. Before she walked into her dad's office, she turned back and looked into my eyes in a meaningful way that I will never forget. I could not believe myself. I simply let her go without saying anything. I let the love of my life go and get married to a guy that she didn't even know. Shame on me!

I drove back to the garage, parked the car, and walked towards the same park. I sat in the same spot as before and cried for hours. But what benefit those tears could bring? Nothing!

That day, on the way back, I left my resignation letter in Sheikh's office along with the key to the car. I had lost her, not even knowing if she loved me back or not. What a coward I was!

I cried and cried for months, but what was done wasn't going to change. I held a grudge towards the stupid traditions of that country, but it was no use. If it hadn't been for the Saudi's tribal and obsolete rules and regulations, perhaps I would have not felt so much pressure when simply expressing my sincere love to a girl. Perhaps I would have been able to express my love in a gradual and natural way instead of having to do it all at once or not at all. I decided that I wanted to leave Saudi Arabia and started applying for studying abroad. I wanted to put everything behind and start over my life in a free country where expressing love to a girl is not a crime.

Eventually, I got a scholarship to pursue a PhD degree. Few months later, and I found myself in an airplane, flying to the state of Texas in United States of America, a country that I knew very little about.

CHAPTER FOUR

That flight I took to Houston was my first experience of flying in an airplane as an adult! It was way better than I expected it to be, apart from that little bit of sickness during takeoff and a brief moment of panic during the landing.

In my mind, I had always pictured the state of Texas as a vast desert with cactuses and cowboys everywhere, which was based on the very reliable western movies I had occasionally glimpsed on the TV back home. During the landing, the screen in front of my seat was showing the view of the land from the airplane camera. Surprisingly, the camera was showing a dense forest instead of a dry desert. I panicked! I thought, *Maybe I took a flight to the wrong destination. I mean, how could Texas be a swampy forest?! It must be a desert!*

I decided to double check the destination with the passenger right next to me. As if they would have turned the plane around to take me to the right destination if this was not Houston! But anyway, before I could verbalize my question in broken English, the pilot announced that the airplane was approaching Houston and asked us to fasten our seatbelts and return our seats to an upright position. I breathed a sigh of relief, sat back tight, and relaxed. Little did I know that was only the beginning of a world of surprises and unknowns ahead of me in this new country.

After arriving in the airport, an international student was already waiting for me outside of the gate. He was sent on behalf of the school to pick me up and bring me to the graduate students' housing, which felt really nice and welcoming. The continuous process of settling in started from that first day and I don't think it ever ended.

In a matter of few days, I became friends with some neighbor students across from my room. We really had ton of fun for two weeks, playing new games such as foosball and poker, and all in all, we shared a lot of laughter and joy. All of that, though, ended later when the semester started. The quantity and difficulty of the courses were just plain overwhelming in graduate school, so all of those friends, including me, suddenly vanished. We could barely see each other anymore because everyone was so focused on the courses.

One day in the second week after my arrival in United States, I was walking from the graduate housing to the school, when I saw a biker cycling towards me. The biker waived his hand and said something that sounded like he was saying my name, Hadi, and I thought in my head, *how does that guy know my name? Have I met him before and did not recognize him? Otherwise, this is a proof America really is the land of opportunities! Only two weeks and I'm already famous here.*

Little did I know that the biker had actually said, "howdy," the Texan expression of greeting. But that wasn't the end of American confusion about my name. It didn't take long to see how surprised people acted when they heard my name, but it was a mystery why. Many of them asked me to repeat the name few times, and in the end, had to ask me to spell it for them. Later, I found out that the way I pronounced my name was the same way the word "hottie" was pronounced. Only then did I understand the surprise on people's faces when they heard my name for the first time. They thought I was introducing myself as a hottie!

After the orientation week, the Department of Engineering officially kicked off the new semester with a big barbeque for the engineering graduate students. It was a picnic-style outdoor lunch right near the Chemical Engineering Department Quad. The picnic was meant to be a social mixer event for new students to get them familiarized with both the faculty and the other students.

When you are new in a different country, you naturally do many silly things, but I'll never forget how embarrassed I was on the day of the picnic. I showed up in a completely formal attire, in a suit and tie I had brought with me from home. You can imagine me wearing that outfit in the heat of the day during summers of Texas. I was sweating like a pig, but in my culture, a formal dress is needed when you meet your professors for the first time; it's considered a sign of respect. But apparently, American academia was different. Everybody there, including most of our faculty members, had shown up in shorts and t-shirts. I was so embarrassed I wanted to generate a black hole right there and immerse myself into a parallel universe where suits and ties in the middle of summer are not considered insane.

It took me a short time to really switch from speaking Arabic all the time and get comfortable with speaking English, but keeping up with the American conversational system was not as easy as I thought. I could recognize most of the English words, but then none of the words made any sense in combination. In addition to their weird, never-ending slangs and idioms, Americans love to refer to certain movies, sports, music, and even sometimes politics in their everyday conversations. For someone like me, having not lived my entire life in United States, it was not easy to keep up with them. For a good amount of time, social mingling for me meant trying to listen and make a sensible meaning out of other people's conversations. I looked like I was listening, but in reality I usually had no clue what they were talking about.

Luckily, I did not have any problem following classes as they were taught in simple English with some technical words I knew. As for social culture, I was slowly but surely learning the new culture and trying to adapt to it.

The first year was extremely busy with many different things. Students were required to pass a qualifier exam after the first year of graduate school, so it was a very hectic time. The qualifier exam is basically a comprehensive test on all aspects of your major and in a way, proving yourselves to the professors. Passing the qualifier exam meant the difference between remaining in the PhD program and having to leave, so it was pretty serious. For international students like me, not passing the qualifier exam meant having to go back home due to the fact that student visa required us to remain full-time students, so pressure for us was even higher.

Qualifier exams could be very tough because you had to be able to answer questions not just on one subject, but from every undergraduate-level engineering course you had taken while earning your Baccalaureate degree. Especially for chemical engineers, it required preparedness in a very wide range of sciences and technologies, ranging from molecular chemistry to heat and fluid transport courses. So we had to study extremely hard; the first year was so demanding that I literally had no time for any social interactions except saying "hi" to people and then immediately doubt if I had remembered their names correctly, or if I had ever even met them before!

I remember days when I felt extremely homesick. It was not easy, not easy at all to live in a country where you had no family or relatives. The first major thing I bought in US with the money I had saved from working in Sheikh's house was a laptop. My favorite thing was to use the online video chat to talk to my family; my mom missed me more than anyone else. It was very common for her to break into tears in the middle of our video chats, or for her voice to change as if she had a frog in her throat. After I left Saudi Arabia, my mom was getting sick over and over again, sometimes for no known reason. She was trying hard to hide how much she missed me so as to not harm my success, but I could see it in her eyes and her voice every time we were video chatting. It was not easy at all for me to see her in that pain; Even though I left my country for a better future for my true love, and my mom was always supportive of my decision to study abroad, she was also a mother with emotions only mothers can understand.

I tried to stay resilient throughout and fight all the challenges with strength. I made every effort to be a great student and researcher, to adapt to the new culture, and to manage my homesickness. And of course, the core of my strength was the hope that all these sacrifices would be my gift of the magi for the love I would meet sometime in future. Through this sacred striving for love, I was becoming a better person. I was building my personality, my soul, my social and financial status to better deserve true love. So whenever I began to lose hope and become overly homesick, the dream of a time when my love's hand would be in mine was enough to restore my motivation, and to overcome the darkness of homesickness and get ready again to fight for love.

After a year of studying laboriously, all the PhD students from my cohort passed their qualifier exams, which was a huge relief. I still had to work hard for the remaining years of my PhD, but not as hard as the first year. I had a new academic goal. I wanted to have the best achievements in my class, but at the same time, graduate in the shortest time possible. It was important to me because, by graduating faster, I was hoping that I could visit my mom sooner—something I couldn't do because of the limitations on my student visa.

Gradually, I was developing deeper friendships with the people around me, one example of which is my friendship with Sarah. Sarah was my classmate in the chemical engineering PhD program. I first met her at the Engineering Department barbeque. Over time, I got to know her on a deeper level and realized she had a kind heart and worthy to be a good friend, so we developed a close friendship rather rapidly. She was about my height, with fair skin, reddish curly hair, and green eyes. It didn't take me long to learn that Sarah had very strong Evangelical Christian beliefs, which was why she always dressed very modestly and conservatively. She had devoted her life to her religious beliefs, or in her own words, "to glorify the Lord."

In the beginning of our friendship, she tried her best to talk me into converting to Christianity. She would frequently invite me to her church or asked me if I wanted to know about Jesus. But after some time, she realized that her trying to instill religion in my life was like trying to carry water in a sieve. My experience of religious oppression in Saudi Arabia—added to the fact that strict Wahhabi beliefs were part of the reason I lost Lila—had made me skeptical of any organized religion. In spite of our differences, we remained really close friends because we both respected each other's views. I admired that Sarah was probably one of the kindest and most thoughtful people I had ever met in America.

Two years had passed after I find some time to develop a social life, but I still had not found anyone who reciprocated my love. Dating, as they do in Western societies, was not a norm in Saudi Arabia and I had no experience with it. I knew that I had to come out of my comfort zone and meet people. I learned from my American friends that one good way to meet people is to figure out what activities you enjoyed doing. In that case, even if you didn't find someone interesting in that place, at least you would enjoy the activity. Obviously just doing the things you like to do is not a guarantee that you will meet someone who will truly love you, but for me, it was a good start to just meet people. So I tried to explore various new activities in order to find hobbies I really enjoyed doing.

Meanwhile, one day Sarah insisted that I should go swing dancing with her. At first, I declined because I didn't think that sounded like something that I would ever be interested in. Having grown up in the Middle East, I thought the only dance ever created was belly dancing, and let me put it this way: my belly wasn't designed for that. But in the end, I convinced myself to give it a shot. So I went with her to a café near the university where the swing dancers met on Saturday nights to dance and socialize. To my surprise, I found out that I really enjoyed it! I never thought I'd say this, but that night I realized dancing can be a language of emotions, only with no words. Seeing the dancing couples on the floor going around hand in hand, shoulder to shoulder, face to face, each pair doing their own thing, was really a moving scene. The dancers collectively seemed to be all a part of a common soul in the arbitrary movements of each individual dancer. Just as a nerd like me would, I thought the dancers collectively looked like molecules, running into each other randomly. It was just beautiful.

Soon, I approached a girl who was standing near the corner, waiting for someone to ask her for a dance. I gave her a heads up that I didn't know anything about this type of dance, but I would love to try it and then asked her if she wanted to dance with me. She kindly accepted and even showed me a few simple moves that I attempted but miserably failed that first time. Nevertheless, that first time going to that café led to the second, third, and many more times. In fact, I became a regular, and after taking some classes, I got really good at it too. It was common to get compliments from girls on my dancing, which I humbly accepted. Truthfully, though, I always wished that I could be dancing with my one and only love rather than a series of strangers and acquaintances.

But as time was flying by, I couldn't help feeling like something wasn't right, although I couldn't pinpoint anything particular. I was socializing as much as I could—as much as my studies allowed me. I was also trying my best to be a gentleman, but in the end, no one seemed to like me. I mean, everyone around me loved to have me as a friend, but nothing more. My style was usually to become friends with people, boys and girls, get to know them, and then if I saw that a girl had the potential for understanding and appreciating true love, I would ask if she wanted to go on a date with me. But for two years after I had started to socialize, every attempt had failed. Sometimes, their response was that they are already seeing someone, sometimes that they had recently broken up with their ex and were not ready for a new dating experience, and sometimes they would tell me outright that they were not attracted to me. I wished that for once, someone would take the time to get to know me—to fall in love with the person I was, rather than rejecting me right off the bat.

I confess those constant rejections were making me more and more frustrated than ever. After a long journey of striving to become better for that love I thought I would meet, now for some unknown reason, I was not even able to find anyone who was interested in me. The worst part of it was that I could not understand at all why this was happening. Was it just a numbers game? Was it that I was physically unattractive? Was there something I did that was not behaviorally attractive in American culture and I was simply not aware of it? I didn't know. The only thing I could say was that it seemed at the time no one was ready for me, every time with a different reason. All I could do was to go out more, hoping that someday I would find someone, but the pessimist in my head always whispered, "isn't it the definition of insanity to repeat the same thing and expect to get different result?"

One day, however, I felt like the curse had finally been broken. One Wednesday night in the middle of June, I decided to go to a new dance venue that I had heard about. It was one of those things that you want to do and you continuously have it in the back of your mind but it never happens, each time for a different silly reason. It was a small tea house in the cozy corner of a midtown block, called Chai Tea House. They had these authentic china cups and I had heard they served the best tasting teas in the area. That night I met Heather for the first time. I was standing on the side, chatting with a friend when I felt a tap on my shoulder from behind. I turned back and saw a good looking blond girl wearing a long black dress. She asked if I wanted to dance with her to the song that was on, and of course I did.

As we were dancing, she was looking into my eyes with a constant smile on her face. As I gazed into her eyes with that first sight, I thought "Damn! She is so gorgeous!" and I instantly fell for her. Dancing with a beautiful girl like her had made me lose my cool, so in order to diffuse the awkwardness of being obviously charmed by her beauty, I asked her about what she did for a living. She answered that question, but I don't remember because I wasn't even listening to what she said. I was captivated by her beauty.

When we finished our dance, I remembered that in a few weeks, our university would be throwing what basically was a prom night for college that was called The Esperanza Night. Normally, Esperanza was only for undergraduate students, but that year they had allowed graduate students to buy a limited number of tickets. So all of a sudden after dancing with her in the café, it crossed my mind that I should just go and ask Heather if she wanted to go with me. I waited a little bit to gather all the courage I had, and even borrow some. Then I went and asked her for a second dance. As we were dancing, I told her about the event and asked her to be my date, and she said yes.

If I say words could not describe the joy I experienced when she said yes, I have not exaggerated much. This to me meant that she liked me as well, and in my head, I extrapolated that thought too far ahead, to a time that we would be a married couple living the dream in our own little house. I thought that after so many years, perhaps I had found someone I could truly love, someone who would love me back too. That instant sparkly sensation couldn't feel any better. I had a beautiful girl to take to my prom. So it was with a lot of joy and excitement that I bought two tickets the next morning.

As a graduate student with such a low income and the high expenses of living in a big American city, I did not own a car at the time, and I was going around using Houston's unreliable public transportation. The first thing I did was to start the arrangements to rent a nice and comfortable car for that night. I wasn't embarrassed of being a low-income student and not having a car, but the idea was to provide Heather a safe, easy, and comfortable ride to the Esperanza. I could tolerate the discomfort of a public bus myself, but when it came to her, I wanted to give her the best I could afford.

Anyway, before the Esperanza Night, I had a lot of preparation going on, but I felt it was more than worth it to make this night great for her. I cleaned the interior and exterior of that car with a lot of care. I went to my favorite hair stylist and got the best looking haircut, dressed up in the nicest suit I had, used some fancy cologne I borrowed so I would look and smell good for her, and then went to a store to pick up the bouquet of red and purple roses mixed with lilies. I had already asked her what color dress she would be wearing so that I could match the color of the flowers I get for her.

When I got to the store, out of pure excitement, I told the florist that I was going to prom for the first time in my life with a girl I really liked. When she heard this, a look of surprise and confusion appeared on her face, but she politely said "Oh, good for you!" I knew the reason for her surprise was that I looked older than a high school kid going to a prom, so maybe she thought I was a freak. I added, "I am from Saudi Arabia and going to grad school here. For the first time, they allowed grad students to participate in the university prom." She was actually a nice lady and she tried to help me even more after hearing that this would be my first prom. She suggested I also get a nice looking corsage for Heather, and then helped me pick really pretty flowers to match her dress. She decorated the corsage with dedication and care—she even fixed a plastic butterfly on the top of the flowers that made it look spectacular.

I drove to Heather's house and planned to get there a quarter earlier, thinking it would be better to be early than late. I waited in the car for a few minutes and then rang the bell. She lived in a small house with her roommate. When she opened the door and saw me with the bouquet of flowers in my hand, she said, "Oh my God, such beautiful flowers—no one has ever brought me flowers like this!" Then she invited me to sit inside until she was ready. Her roommate joined us in the living room too and she introduced me to her. While she was finding a vase to put the flowers in them, she was telling her roommate about how beautiful the flowers were. From that big smile on her face, it was clear she really appreciated my efforts.

Anyway, she was ready about half an hour or so after I got seated in the living room of her house. She came out in the beautiful long black dress she was wearing with her long blond hair done so nicely. I gave her the corsage and we then walked out and got into the car.

When we got into the car, I asked her what kind of food she was in mood for that night. I didn't want to pick a restaurant on my own because I wanted to take her wherever she liked. She asked "Are we going to a normal restaurant or a luxury one?" I, of course, said we can go wherever you like, and I meant it. Even though paying a big bill in a fancy restaurant wasn't something that a poor student like me would really look forward to, I wanted to live by my values as a true lover, and seeing the happiness of my beloved meant my own happiness.

We went to a super fancy restaurant she knew nearby, which cost me a hundred and fifty dollars for two of us for a plate of salad and fish that we could've gotten elsewhere for fifty bucks, tops. That probably was the most expensive dinner I have ever had, but I was honestly glad she was enjoying it.

So after dinner, I drove her to the prom venue on university campus. Since she and I had already met through dancing, we both really pulled it off great. Our dancing skills made us the center of attention for a while. It was a good night of dancing, laughing, and fun.

When we headed out to the parking lot to get in the car and go home, we were laughing and chatting, then all of sudden, I realized the full moon in the sky, and I suggested we both sit on a grassy hill and watch the moon for a while. It was here that I did something I never had done before: I kissed a girl for the first time in my life, at the age of twenty-four!

I had been holding her hand in mine for a while, looking at the night sky, so when I felt like I wanted to kiss her, I squeezed her hand gently and turned my face from looking at the sky to her face, and paused for a second or so. She turned her face to look at me: my eyes staring into her eyes, a smile on her face and mine. I moved my face towards hers as slowly as I could; her face had become the most gorgeous face in the planet in my eyes. As my face was approaching hers in the slowest way, she closed her eyes and approached me. Our lips met halfway. Just a small touch of our lips and then we pulled away for a moment. We opened our eyes looking at each other, and then leaned in and kissed again. When I paused, she moved closer and continued it with passion. That was a very relaxing moment because all of the previous doubt I had in the back of my mind whether or not she really liked me romantically went away with our sensual kiss. After we had been kissing for a while, she suggested that it was getting late and we should go back, so we made our way towards the car to go home.

On the way to her home, we had a great conversation about a bunch of random topics, but our dialogue was so natural and smooth. She told me that it was strange that she felt so comfortable and at ease with me so quickly, which was so nice to hear because I took it as a compliment on my honest love.

We went on a few more dates after that. One night, I invited her to a Middle Eastern restaurant. She was trying some of those Middle Eastern foods for the first time in her life, and she really liked them. We then went for a little walk in nearby areas and just by random chance we found an area with really big houses and peacocks hanging around. She just loved it! She told me she was from Georgia and they had peacock farms there in her hometown too, so that scene was very enjoyable for her. Then totally unplanned, I asked if she wanted to get some ice cream, but it was too late for ice cream shops to be open, so we went to a grocery store and grabbed some bulk ice cream, got some spoons from the counter and started to dig in. When I could see a hint of smile on her lips or a slight shine of happiness in her eyes, it was the biggest prize I could ever win.

Just when I thought I might actually have found someone with a mutual love, something terrible happened in the most shocking way. It was our fifth date and we were having a blast: a ton of laughing, and kissing, but when the night was over and I was walking her to her car, she asked me if she could be honest with me, and then she said she was not interested in me!

I could not believe what I heard with my own ears. Ten minutes ago, she was kissing me passionately for the fifth date and now all of a sudden she was saying that she was not interested in me. I was shocked, as if I was hit in the head by a heavy weight, confused as hell, lost in the fear that this beautiful feeling was all nothing but a mirage.

We were both standing in front of her car. In total shock, I asked her if I did anything wrong unintentionally that made her upset, but she said no, the dates were just fine. So the cycle of me trying to guess the reason and her refusing to give me a straight answer began. Meanwhile, it abruptly started raining and we took shelter under the balcony of a restaurant facing that parking lot. I was begging her not to stop this beautiful thing we had, to give me another chance to start over and compensate for the mistakes I may have made that even I myself didn't know, but she said "the more you ask to start over, the more I know I have made the right decision to end it," then she said she wanted to go home; it was getting late.

I said, "I am going to just stay here under the balcony for a while. You do what you want to do, but I'm not going to walk away from someone I like so much." *Not once again after I walked away from Lila*, I thought. She asked "So what are you going to do? Stay here the rest of the night?" I said, "No I will leave too sooner or later, but I'm not going to be the one who walks off and leaves you." Then she carelessly walked away, saying only one word without looking back: "Bye." With that, she got in her car and drove away. I stood there for about an hour, just watching rain and going over what happened in my head. I was in deep shock. A while back, I thought I was the happiest man on earth. I thought I had found someone who really made me happy; I thought I had found true love, but then all of a sudden that sandcastle of dreams I made for myself and felt so safe and proud in it crashed right in front of me and I didn't even know how. Finally, I left the patio of that restaurant and went home, wondering what the hell happened.

I let few days pass; I had to get over the deep shock of that night to be able to think clearly, but I wanted to know what exactly I did wrong and ask her to give me just one more chance to correct that mistake. I had decided to not give up until she agreed to give me another chance. I thought I should not give up on it so easily just like I did on Lila; after all, I thought I had finally found love with Heather.

After a few days, I called her. I expected her not to pick the phone up after how easily she left me, but she actually got the phone on the first try. I tried to be calm and not too emotional and just look for the reason why this happened. I had only one question for her and asked that over and over again, "I want to know why. How come after the fifth date, you suddenly realized you were not attracted to me? To know if you are attracted to someone or not doesn't take that long, so I want to know what the real reason is and if I can do anything to change it."

She did not want to give any particular reason, but I really insisted and repeated myself for the third time that I needed to know what the real reason was. Then she suddenly became quiet; I could only hear her breathing on the phone line, which was heavier than usual. From that heavy, nervous breath and the moments of pause, it seemed like she was considering whether to answer my question. She then abruptly broke her silence and said, "Hadi, the real reason is kind of cruel. Are you really sure you want to hear it?"

Her warning made me pause for a second, but then I thought I didn't care how cruel the reason was; I'd rather know. So I said, "Yes, I am sure. Tell me what the real reason is, please."

She continued, "There are some decisions in life that aren't easy to talk about, but I'm not ashamed of any of my actions.

So, know that it is not because of your persistence that I am telling you this! I am an independent human with free will and I don't really have to explain myself to anyone if I don't want to, but I'm brave enough to express myself the way I am. Is that clear?"

I said, "Yes, it is!"

After a short pause, she then continued, "It was almost two years ago. I was a junior student at a small community college. Life was really good. Courses were tough, but I really enjoyed learning, so the student life was amazing. As the next step, I was planning to transfer to a better university to pursue psychology, the major I always wanted to study. Everything in my life was fine until I met my ex-boyfriend in college who stole my heart. The first time we met was in the Psychology 102 course we were both taking. The moment I saw him, it was like my brain stopped and my heart took control of my every single action. I was so awkward around him with a big creepy smile on my face. I even lost the ability to talk properly. My obsession with him was growing over time. Gradually, I got so obsessed with him that I could not eat or sleep well; all I thought of was him. I didn't know what, but something about him was so unique and magical. I just had this enormous crush on him, but didn't even have the guts to tell him.

Eventually, after about a month, I got my act together and asked him if he wanted to grab coffee with me, and he said yes! I could not contain myself in my skin; I was so happy I wanted to burst into dust and fly over the whole world. On our first date, I realized we also had so much in common: we both liked the same Rock bands, we both loved hiking and video games, and we both were cat people—those might seem like little things, but it was like he was my soulmate. We dated for a year as boyfriend and girlfriend. Everything felt just so phenomenal and magical. In hindsight, though, there were many signs I should have paid attention to, but my feelings for him were making me neglect or rationalize all of those red flags. The crush I had on him was making me blind to any of his faults. I actually picked a fight with my best friend when she tried to tell me about how fake this guy was, and I accused my best friend of being jealous of me. He had become my prince on a white horse.

I was all in for him. I was seeing my present and future in him. However, after a while I realized even though I loved him more than I had ever loved anyone, he was not supporting me or giving me the mental and physical attention I desired. As a woman, I wanted my man to be my rock in return for all the love I gave him.

At that point, I interrupted her to ask, "What do you mean he did not support you? Can you give some examples?"

She answered, "No, I'm not comfortable sharing the details of my personal life with you. It's enough to know he wasn't giving me what I needed in a relationship."

That response made me even more curious, so I asked, "Okay, that's fine if you don't want to share details, but what do you mean "in return"? That kind of sounds like a word we use when we want to exchange goods and services. Is that all a relationship is to you—an exchange?"

She answered in a slightly offended voice, "Call it whatever you want. I don't really care. I know you have these high-level ideas about love, but in reality, a relationship is nothing but a bunch of compromises. You give something and in return you get something else."

I was shocked by that answer, but she seemed defensive, and so I chose not to continue down that road with her. She noticed my silence and continued her story, "The more unsupportive and indifferent he became; the more love I was offering him. I was doubling down on my selfless giving to him because that dependent and weak Heather wanted to feel like she was good enough for him. My biggest fear was losing him and his attention. At one point, he even asked me to stop studying and go work with him in a restaurant where he was waiting tables. He told me he wanted to save money for our wedding. Delusional as I was, I dropped out of community college and joined him to work in the restaurant.

One day at work, though, I felt nauseated and threw up in the restroom. At first, I thought it was the pressure of the long hours I was working, but it happened repeatedly. It turned out, it wasn't fatigue... I was pregnant. It was his baby. The moment I saw the positive sign on the pregnancy test, immediately I felt a deep love for this unborn child. I dreamed of a time in the future when we would all live together in our own house. Having a child with the love of my life was a beautiful gift.

The night after the pregnancy test was positive, I planned to break the news to him in the most romantic way. I made him spaghetti, his favorite food, and purchased a bottle of ten-year-old chardonnay with my savings.

That night, soon after opening the conversation, I realized that he did not want to keep the child and did his best to convince me to abort it. I never wanted to do that; I was already feeling an emotional bond with this unborn baby. That child was the result of making love to someone I wanted so badly, not to mention God wouldn't forgive me for killing a baby.

From that night, everything turned dark and sad. Almost every night we had a fight. He became overly aggressive. To make me to abort the baby, he would use any tactics from sweet talking to shouting. I kept resisting him, but he wouldn't stop trying to convince me that I should abort the baby. Finally, he told me I had to choose between keeping the baby and seeing him. Unfortunately, out of the fearing of losing him, I eventually gave in to his demands and aborted my innocent baby. I thought this was the only way to keep him in my life. The truth is, right after I had the abortion, that bastard left and never answered my phone calls. I had lost him forever. I had left my school, ruined my future, and terminated the life of an innocent child because of a stupid crush, a deep desire to love someone who didn't deserve a bit of it.

My failed relationship with him made me hate all men, especially the ones who claim to be nice guys. When I saw you on the dance floor and saw how emotional you became with each and every love song the DJ played, I thought I had found another victim for my revenge. I saw how you fell for me at the first sight. I know how to use my beauty to make men do things for me and give me whatever I want. I know how to play tricks on their shallow minds to swindle them out of their money to bankruptcy and nothing makes me happy like that revenge.

But in your case, gradually and to my disbelief, you showed me that not all men are untrustworthy. Even though your first look at me was shallow, you were putting your heart into it. You really and genuinely believe in the true love you talk about, and you act on it wholeheartedly.

I interrupted her and said, "Thanks for noticing that, but how can you know my intentions after just a handful of dates?"

"Do you really want to pull on that thread? You know it's not too late to change my mind about that, right?" She responded with a bitter laughter.

She continued, "But in all seriousness, I think I have seen enough to give you the benefit of the doubt. I could see how you went out of your way for me even when I was being intentionally difficult. There is a real purity and honesty in your actions."

She continued, "I felt ashamed that I was trying to play you. If I wasn't already so hurt, I would have probably fallen in love with you because of who you are, but I had initiated everything with intention to play with your emotions, so the best I could do was to let you off the hook. You deserve better than me, Hadi."

Then she breathed a sigh of relief and continued, "God knows how difficult it was to admit everything, but there it is— the truth you wanted to know. My advice to you is to learn from my mistakes and only give your unconditional love to someone who deserves it. That person is not necessarily the same person who gives you those magical warm and fuzzy feelings. I had to learn this the hard way, but now you don't. Good luck with your life, Hadi," and then she hung up.

After that phone call, I never called Heather again, nor went to that dance venue. Frankly, I was upset and disappointed but mainly very confused as to what happened between us. My scientific background compelled me to identify the root cause of the past events. I knew her side of the story now, but from my side, I could not understand at all why the relationship ended that way even though I really tried to act by my principles of true love. I didn't hesitate a second if there was something I could do to make her happy. I selflessly tried to love her, so why did it not work? I was confused.

Why did she choose me in the first place? Am I just an easy target to be manipulated? What could I have done differently if anything? Maybe, I should have first got to know her deeper before falling in love with her pretty face, I thought in my head in the days following the break-up. But after a few days, the thoughts in my head weren't only about that particular experience, but rather a more general question had tingled my sense of curiosity. In fact, that sad and rapid break-up with Heather had made me think about the general concept of love on a much deeper level than before.

I started reading many good books on this topic. These books taught me many useful communication techniques I could use, but I thought there was something more fundamental about true love that was not covered, something that was so deep in our souls. I realized that many of these books did not discuss the mindsets in romantic relationships and only use assumptions about our mindsets. But mindsets have such an essential role in what we do, so there was room for someone to analyze the mindsets that govern our romantic relationships with the nuances of modern life in mind.

I started to think really deeply about that subject. One way to start was by analyzing how I fell for Heather. If I was being honest with myself, the basis for my interest in her was really that initial spark I felt when I saw how beautiful she was. Even though I did my best to act selflessly after I had fallen for her, the foundation for my love was an instant feeling that happened in the first few seconds I met her, a spark per se, very similar to how Heather had fallen for her ex-boyfriend. I started to wonder if my feeling for Heather was true love or was it just a spark? Thinking deeply about Heather's advice gave me another clue as to what went wrong. Her advice to offer my pure unconditional love only to someone who deserves it was a clue to the fact that by letting myself fall for her external beauty so quickly, I had not considered her intentions or mindsets. Perhaps the problem for many people was that they fell in love with someone whose very definition of love could be extremely different than theirs, if not opposite.

I compared it to when I loved Lila. My love for Lila was of a much deeper one. It is true that I had a crush on her when we were younger children, but I didn't let myself fall in love quickly. I loved Lila not because her dad was rich nor because of how hot she was, but only when I realized she also firmly believed in a mutual selfless type of love. Only then, the crush for Lila turned into love for her in my mind.

I came to the conclusion that in order to find true love, we must first purify our own intentions and mindsets. Over time, I identified that relationships of our day and age are based on four fundamental mindsets of spark, fear, exchange, and egoless love. I hypothesized that only a mutual egoless mindset can lead to true love many of us are looking for. This kind of mutual selflessness could lead to a true love, just like the one I had read in the story of "The Gift of the Magi."

During the next 6 months, my deep thinking had made me much more conscientious about what love is and what it is not, so I thought of sharing it with others. *Why not open a student club where I can promote the idea of egoless love to others and create a community for those who are interested in learning more about love?* I thought to myself. A while after, I set up a new student community and called it the Egoless Love Club.

CHAPTER FIVE

W hen I decided to initiate a student club, called the Egoless Love Club, I knew it was going to be a lot of work, but I hoped it would be worth the effort. It was supposed to be a club devoted to the study, appreciation, and promotion of true love as well as support to those who seek it.

Anyone who has managed any student activity before knows that it is extremely time- and energy-demanding, at least in the beginning. For a few months, I spent a huge chunk of my spare time organizing and promoting the club.

I was looking to hopefully find some students who didn't care only about grades and parties, but also cared about becoming better people through love. Of course, I was open to anyone who even slightly believed in the idea of true love; anyone who wanted to help to the cause.

So to spread the word to students about the club and what it intended to do, I designed a bunch of flyers. Wherever I could find a crowd of students, I would gather all my courage and approach them to hand over these flyers and hopefully talk about its mission. Unfortunately, though, I wasn't extremely successful at selling the idea. A couple of months passed and not a single soul signed up for the club, but I kept trying anyway.

One day when I was standing on the sidewalk with flyers in hand, Justin bumped into me. Justin was a graduate student majoring in music. He was in the class of 2013, two years ahead of me, but he was in no rush to finish school. I had briefly met Justin before, in one of the student social events, but this particular day was the beginning for a series of interesting—though sometimes frustrating—conversations.

No doubt, Justin was among the most popular kids at the university. Actually, he was beyond popular; he was a super star, especially among ladies, to the extent that his friends had given him the nickname "chick-magnet." He was worshiped by many students like the demigod of shallow pleasures and casual life-style. Party-animal is an understatement when explaining Justin's character. He was the emperor of the crazy parties in the school because there was literally no limit for what could be done at his house parties. His dad, being a well-known Texan multi-millionaire, had bought him a big, modern house adjacent to our university campus. He had more than enough money to quench the thirst among college kids for the craziest parties and that's how he had gained his fame.

His popularity wasn't all because of his hip life-style and crazy parties, but also due to his extremely charming behavior and handsome appearance. He was above six feet tall and had lean but strong muscles, not to mention his six-pack abs that made girls go crazy. His piercing blue eyes were the most prominent feature of his face; they would remind you of a kind and loyal puppy. He grew his blond hair long and kept his beard perfectly trimmed.

When he saw me with the flyers in hand, he stopped walking and said in a voice that seemed like he was at least a bit drunk, "Yo, dude! Was it Hadie? Hodi? ...Uh, it was Holi, right?"

"Hello Justin! How have you been? It's Hadi! It's pronounced like Audi, the car, but with an H in the beginning," I said while smiling.

He said, "Sorry man! I can't remember names, but your face looks totally familiar."

I said, "Yeah, we briefly met at the little social event after the student talent contest last semester. I would be surprised if you could remember my name!"

He said, "Yeah, sure man! So where're you from?"

This is a typical question any foreigner with even a slightly non-American accent would get in America, so being used to it, I answer quickly, "Saudi Arabia!"

He said, "Cool! So what are you up to right now?"

I briefly explained to him that I have initiated a student club on campus with the goal to promote true love. I tried to explain further about egoless love mindset and how I aimed to help people achieve it, that he interrupted me with an annoyed sigh, "Wow! I'm not trying to be rude, bro, but this ain't gonna do shit for you! You gotta get your gaming skills up and running; you know what I'm saying? At least, some pick-up lines or something. That's the way to score chicks, buddy. Not this pile of bullshit!" he said with a stoic face.

Up to that point, I had gotten all sorts of unpleasant reactions from the students on campus. The most common reaction was to totally ignore me. Even if they stopped briefly, it wasn't uncommon for them to imply that they didn't have time, or interest. But without a doubt, no other reaction was as offensive, humiliating, and rude as this one! Scoring chicks?! Does he think of women as trophies or think of love as a competition?! Did he just dare to call my sacred true love a "pile of bullshit"?!

That wasn't the best first impression anyone could ever give me. His words were deeply offensive and even disgusting, but quickly, I reminded myself that I was there to help other people discover true love and listening to them patiently, no matter how difficult, was the first part of that process. By being there, I had chosen to be open to hearing points that could completely contradict with the true love I believed in. So I calmed myself and asked him, "Are you saying honest love can never work?"

He said, "Duh! Of course not, everyone knows that. Girls and boys want completely different things in life. Girls want lots of emotional shit, and the only thing guys care about is sex, but we don't tell the girls that. No way! That's why as a man, you should learn how to trick girls. All guys do it to some extent; tricking girls is a survival skill you need as a guy throughout your life. The main idea behind it is to know how they think and use it to your advantage. It's like hunting. The first rule of hunting is to know your prey better than you know yourself. The key is to show and tell them exactly what they want to see or hear. It doesn't matter if you're faking it, you just have to make them believe you have whatever it is that they fall for.

Just look how honesty has worked out for you. Do you know how you actually look to girls by talking about true love? It sounds to them like you are a desperate loser, and that's not the image they want to have in their mind from their Mr. Right. That's why this ain't gonna work, man!"

Obviously, I was a million times more frustrated than before, but I kept on listening and trying to somehow understand his point of view, so I said, "Well, I'm not desperate, or a loser, or really looking for sex! I can't even imagine how anyone would want sex without truly loving the other person, but still I would like to know more about your perspective if you have some time to talk."

He scratched his head, paused for a couple of seconds, and then said, "You know what? I'm gonna cover you, bro! Why don't you show up tomorrow night for the party at my house, and I'll teach you a thing or two. Oh, and give me your digits! I'm gonna text you the address for the party later today." After getting my number, he walked away. Later that night, he sent me the time and the address for his party.

So the following night, I showed up at Justin's house party, which quite expectedly was a crazy one! The craziest and most exaggerated college party I had seen in the movies was like a church service compared to what I saw at Justin's house that night. Without wanting to go to too much detail, I can summarize the whole craziness into three clauses: lots of alcohol, lots of drugs, and lots of nudity.

After a little bit of wandering around in the house, I found Justin lying on a couch with a couple of half-naked girls, taking turns sniffing lines of a white powder that were on the coffee table in front of them. He said he would catch up with me later. Even though the crazy nature of the party was making me feel like a fish out of water, I was still trying to chat with the guests and enjoy myself as much as possible. My main goal in going to that party was to talk to Justin, and I was waiting for a proper opportunity to do so.

As I was hanging around the house, I suddenly recognized one of my classmates in the living room. He was smoking a cigar with bunch of other people, so I joined them to socialize. I introduced myself to everyone in that circle of people. The last person in the circle was tightly hugging one of the girls who seemed to be wearing bikinis, but on a closer look, it turned out to be body painting, making them totally nude. When I introduced myself to him, he said his name was Adrien.

That name rang a bell. On a few occasions, Sarah had brought her boyfriend's name up, Adrien, but we had never got a chance to actually meet.

Could this be Sarah's boyfriend? I was wondering in my head, so I asked him if he knew Sarah Wellington.

As soon as I mentioned Sarah's name, Adrien got anxious, vaguely mumbled something that sounded like an excuse, and then abruptly got out of there. It was strange, but I gave him the benefit of the doubt.

After a while, Justin climbed on a table and howled, "Aooohooooooh!" By doing this, he caught almost everyone's attention, and then yelled in an ascending tone, "Alright! Who's ready for some live music?"

Everyone cheered and applauded.

He sat on the kitchen bar facing the living room and started playing guitar and singing at the same time. It was truly a beautiful piece of music. I knew he was music major, but I didn't imagine him to be so talented at it. After his solo performance, other music students joined him and their band played for a couple of hours.

It was a little after midnight and the party was still alive and on as if no one felt any need to take a rest, which made me felt like a grandpa! I was exhausted, but at the same time, I didn't want to leave without talking to Justin. The weather outside was not bad at all, so I sat on a swing on the porch and started thinking about Justin's lifestyle, trying to put myself in his shoes in the hope of better understanding him, especially when it came to love.

The train of my thought was broken when he opened the door and yelled, "There you are!" He was drunk as a skunk and high as the sky. Seeing all that when he walked on the porch, I doubted that this was the right time to have any sort of emotional or intellectual conversation with this guy, but I was there anyway, so I went with the flow. I said, "Thanks for inviting me to your party. I really liked your music."

He reached his pocket, pulled out a cigarette and asked if I have a light, but I didn't smoke. He looked around to find a light. He finally lit his cigarette and sat on one of the wooden chairs on the porch. He said, "Come on, man! Join me around the table! Let the master begin his teachings!"

I got off the swing and joined him at the wooden table. I sat right in front of him.

He said, "Tell me! What brought you here to this party?"

I said, "Remember? Yesterday? On Campus?"

He laughed out loud and said, "I was just messing with you!" Being under the influence, he continued to laugh his pants off for a minute or so until he kind of ran out of breath. Then he said, "Alright man. Let me ask you a question: You saw all those kids in the party, huh? Some were here for free drinks, some for drugs, and some for hookers, but what do you think they are all fucking looking for?"

I said, "I don't know. Fun?"

He continued, "Exactly, my man! They all wanna have fun! Have you heard the expression, as long as you are happy, or whatever floats your boat?"

I said, "Many times!"

He continued, "In life, all we want is pleasure. It doesn't

matter how the hell we get it; at the end, we all just wanna feel fucking good! All the time! This is the key shit you are forgetting about a lot of people. You are putting yourself to so much trouble to live a life that you call true love. People don't want anything that is hard, and that's why what you're doing is fucking getting you nowhere into girls' pants!"

Once again, I was disgusted by his words; I was disgusted by how he looked at love as if it was another means of satisfying his every whim, yet I was reminding myself that I was no one to judge him; I was reminding myself that I was there to better understand the opposing mindsets. I kept quiet and calm.

He continued, "Look, bro! Let me break it down for you: Love is a market. Just like any other thing in our life. In this market, everyone is looking for the goods that make them happy, the goods possessing all or most of the qualities they desire. Those qualities people look for may not always be the same, but you'll be fucking surprised how similar they are. Girls look for emotions and relationships, and guys look only for sex. We don't give a damn about the fancy flowers or sweet chocolates we buy for them, or the gooey shit we tell them every now and then. Those are all just marketing techniques that help us get what we want: to get into their pants!"

He threw away his cigarette butt, lit another one, and continued, "Women like tall guys with lean muscles, manly jaws and symmetrical faces; guys who are well-dressed and live large. Someone just like the handsome man you are looking at right now! Women want guys who are strong outside but at the same time soft and flexible inside. Now, they might not have a fucking clue how they fall in love, but they do it based on their interpretation of what strong and kind is. One girl may see the strength in the shape of your face or your physique; another may find it in you being rich or generous. They may find it in the muscles you are building or the career you have. It takes less than five seconds for a girl to decide whether she wants you or not, just five seconds—think about it, man! Now, a smart guy like me knows what he wants in this market and goes for it, and again, what we all want is…?"

He paused for a few seconds to see if I say what he wants me to say, but after seeing no reaction from me, he continued, "Sex! It's in our nature, man. It's evolution. We have no choice over it. So a smart guy adapts and learns how to fake it. I hope you fucking appreciate these lessons I'm giving you for free! This can change your life into a heaven where you can get any girl you want. It's simple, my man! Just like a good hunter who puts out bait for his prey, you should know what girls look for in this market of love and provide them with exactly that."

I said, "And what if you don't have what they are looking for in this so-called market of love?"

He laughed and said, "Bro, are you really a PhD student? I already told you! That's easy-peasy. You just fake it; you give them an illusion of what they are looking for, and almost always they fall for it. You keep the illusion alive for them as long as you are getting what you want from them; but when you get tired? No worries at all. Just move on to the next one."

I asked, "Do you think this is fair? I mean they probably get heartbroken when they realize they got manipulated, right?"

He answered with a shrug, "Maybe, but that's what any market is about. It's nobody's fault, man. That's the shit they signed up for by being so shallow. Let me tell you something from my own life. My grandpa immigrated to the United States from Germany like a hundred years ago and bought a farmland, then what happened? Jackpot! His farmland ended up being one of the sweetest oil fields in Texas, so you guess he was super rich, right? Now, my dad is way richer compared to even my grandpa! He has been a Wall Street guy for two decades, and he got even richer than his own dad, and he didn't do that by being fair to people. His advice for me when I was growing up was simple: 'In life, some people lose for others to win; just always be the one who wins, not the one who loses.' Now, love or any other thing in our fucking life is the same shitty concept—it's just a marketplace where we all try to get what we want and all that matters is winning."

At that moment, he abruptly got up from his chair, went inside, and came back with a bottle of bourbon, two glasses, and a bucket full of ice cubes. He offered me a shot, but I politely refused and he didn't insist. He then poured a drink in his glass, lit another cigarette and said, "Ha! I've tried every drink and drug you could imagine, but nothing is as good as bourbon on the rocks with a cigarette, nothing man! You don't know what you're missing."

I felt like we were getting distracted from the topic of interest, so I immediately asked another question, "So I'm curious, what percentage of people do you think select their loved ones with this love-market mentality that you are talking about?"

He stared at me as if I badly disappointed him. After an awkward silence, he said, "Are you fucking kidding me? Everyone does that! You are the only fucking man I have ever seen who believes this bullshit of true love. What the hell do you even mean? I read in the flyer you gave me that you believe true lovers should like their loved ones as much as themselves? Who in their right mind would want to do such stupid shit?"

I reflected inside for a minute and said with a humble voice, "You see, when couples truly love each other, they form a unified soul who is greater than each individual, and yes, they love that unified soul more than themselves, and as such they let go of selfishness. They love their beloved more than themselves! This is a genuine, honest, and deep love. True lovers do love with minimum expectations, if any. I know you probably think I'm crazy for saying this. I know at least I believe in true love wholeheartedly. So not only do I think true love is not fake, but also believe those who fake it will not achieve true love."

He leaned forward, put his both arms on the table, and continued, "Look, man. What you are offering in this market, this true love, is worth nothing to others. You heard me right: nothing! Zero! Most girls, knowingly or unknowingly, select their partners based on that first spark. That's when you make a girl go *wow*! When you make her feel like there is something very special about you. Now it doesn't need to be genuine, but the spark needs to be there for them to like you. Some people just naturally have what it takes in the market to be popular. It's a combination of right type of body, nice outfit, and the type of behavior women like. Now like I said, there are slight variations from girl to girl or from guy to guy, but I guarantee you buddy, the qualities people look for in this market are so similar that an asshole like me who knows exactly how to fake it can get any girl he wants, and leaves people like you with no chance!"

He poured another drink of bourbon for himself and continued, "There's a saying: nice guys finish last. Let me fucking tell you nice guys finish when everybody else is done with their job! So rule number one of this market is this: being nice doesn't get you girls! Be savage, be tricky, be fake, but whatever you do, be exactly what girls want! You gotta be eye-catching; you gotta be their fantasy prince on a white horse coming from far away to save them! Make them feel like you are going to treat them like a princess; but always remember, it's a market! As soon as they buy all that shit from you, you are going to get what guys all really want! Fucking sex!"

Abruptly, I interrupted him by saying in a firm and angry voice, "But sex is not the only thing I want! Look! I'm a man too, but empty sex is nothing compared to the deep meaning true love gives me!" I couldn't listen to one more word of what he was saying! Everything he said was an insult to those boys and girls who truly believe in the sacredness of love and live by it. Now maybe there aren't so many of us in this day and age, but even so, those who really believe in love still stand by honest and true love every day and second of their lives! And a handsome jerk like him was an insult to all of us.

"Oh, so you are saying you don't like sex, and you expect me to believe that? Or maybe you're still a virgin?" he said, laughing out loud.

He was making me lose my patience. He was twisting what I said in favor of his own point. I answered even more angrily, "No! That's not what I said. I am a human being and I probably enjoy sex as much as all other people, but I never even dare to fake love just to get sex. How can a lover be so needy? Loving is giving. There is a difference between what you're talking about, which is being needy, and what I'm talking about, which is having needs. Your mentality of marketplace of love is all about what you get and want. The mentality I have on the other hand, is not about what I get at all; it is about how I can make my love happier, no matter what it costs me. Do you understand the difference?"

He poured his third drink since our conversation started, lit another cigarette, and said, "What the hell, man? The question is not whether I understand your fictional true love— it is if you fucking understand the reality of how people fall in love. You can live your life based on whatever mumbo jumbo philosophy you want, but the reality of how people fall in love is through that first spark. They shop around to find a girlfriend or boyfriend, just like they shop around in any other marketplace."

Standing up from the chair, he continued in a slow, slurring voice, "Let me give you an example so that maybe you see the facts better: Take a good look at me, bro! I belong to a very rich family. What does that mean for girls? Think about it? They see I can treat them nicely—give them whatever they want! I throw parties at my house at least four times a month. I give them laughs, lots of fun, and good times. Can you do that for them? Hell no! Oh, and because I'm rich, I don't need to waste my time actually studying. Instead, I'm a very relaxed dude who doesn't care about life much and this gives girls a sense of trust, freedom, and peace. But what about you? Just a boring nerd! You think girls will let go of those sparks and listen to your nonsense true love? I have my own rock band that reminds girls of their fantasies, but do you even play harmonica? And by the way, I know how to fake the role of a polite gentleman when I'm dealing with girls. Looks like a complete package, doesn't it? These are the qualities that attract girls and create a spark in their hearts. They would never leave qualities I have for a guy like you who believes in a fictional true love! You get it now?"

Throughout the conversation with him, I tried really hard to be patient and understand his intentions and points, regardless of his language and without judging his personality. Yet, at that point, I felt like I'd had enough of it. I felt like this conversation would not add any more understanding of his views, and I needed to respect my own feelings and beliefs by stopping the conversation.

I simply got up from the chair and walked down the stairs of the porch and politely said, "Alright! This conversation is over! Thanks for inviting me to your party though."

He got up and tried to walk off the stairs, but he was so drunk and high that he wasn't able to walk those few steps down. So he shouted, "Look man! I was only trying to help you score some chicks! Go! Get fucking lost! Loser!" and then he went back inside. I walked back to my apartment as well.

A few weeks passed. One Monday morning, an email announcement was sent to the entire university from the dean's office. It was an official statement informing us that dozens of students had experienced drug overdose at a student party the night before, and that some of them were hospitalized and in critical conditions. The email specified that according to the police report, they were all using the same batch of drugs provided by the host.

This was most likely one of Justin's house parties! He was obviously in serious trouble now!

CHAPTER SIX

Pretty quickly, the news about the drug-overdose spread even beyond the university. The names of the students who were involved remained confidential per school's policy, but most students knew this was one of Justin's big parties. Who else was throwing huge parties like that? Almost fifty students had been hospitalized, so the stakes were high.

At least not until later, the majority of students couldn't have cared less about the news! To them, it was just another crazy college memory. But school officials were taking the incident quite seriously for a very obvious reason: publicity! The story had found its way to the local television, podcasts, and social media, creating a public relations nightmare for the school. Seeing their donation dollars at risk, the executive heads of our university reacted with strict new rules: For a few months, there would be no parties allowed on-campus. Students involved in any written or verbal referral to use or exchange of illegal drugs were threatened to extreme disciplinary measures. The school honor council was firmly reviewing the case of the students involved in Justin's party. As for Justin himself, he was immediately dismissed from the school.

All those college kids who were making fun of the whole thing soon realized this was serious! It got serious for them because it meant their nightly smoking fun was at risk, which was considered a disaster for the pot-heads, of course. I don't really think a high percentage of students were doing heavy drugs, but for sure, weed was really popular. In some cases, weed had replaced U.S. Dollars as the common currency among students. For instance, I remember seeing a post on Facebook from a college girl offering weed in return for help moving her furniture out of her room! Unbelievable for me, but true story!

So that accident gradually made life a bit more difficult for some kids at school, at least temporarily. But very honestly, I didn't care at all. I heard other students talking about it every now and then, but I had more important things to do, a dream to fulfill. I never felt the need to drug myself to feel good or passionate. I was passionate about my dream of true love.

A few months passed. Despite the random success I had in finding some students who were willing to participate in the Egoless Love Club's activities and events—thanks to the free pizza I occasionally provided—I was still unsuccessful in finding my own love. I had been socializing, developing friendships, and even praying, but nothing seemed to work. It was frustrating, but at the same time, I didn't want to rush it. I tried my best not to fall for pretty faces this time, but to find a girl who would appreciate my love. Every once in a while, I would ask a girl out, but soon I would be rejected. Their reasons for this rejection varied, but some typical answers were, "Oh, sorry, but I am very busy and have no time!" or "Oh, I'm sorry but I just recently broke up with my ex and I'm not ready to seriously date a new guy!" or the most direct answer: "Oh, I'm sorry but I don't feel attracted to you! I would love to remain a friend though." Of course, I appreciated friendship, but I wanted love—true love—more than anything else. My biggest confusion stemmed from the fact that I did not know for sure why I was getting rejected. *Was it just luck? Was it a behavior of mine I wasn't aware of? Was it my appearance? Was it the fact that I was an immigrant? I often wondered.*

Over time, my failure to find anyone who could love me for who I was made me think maybe Justin was right. Well, surely I believed he wasn't right about many things, but maybe he was right about one thing: not many people cared about the deep love I had to offer, or even all the lifelong sacrifices and efforts I had made for that one and only love of my life. Maybe I just wasn't hot enough for them. It wasn't that I believed looks should not matter at all—no, there should certainly be some level of attraction between a couple in a relationship, but it felt like many people only based their relationships on whether or not they have that immediate first spark towards the other person, just like Justin said. Maybe who I was on the outside wasn't eye-catching enough for them so none of them cared about who I was inside. Or maybe I just had to continue my search and hope that one day, I would find the right match.

I was coming from a country in the Middle-East, and that wasn't helping either. They would turn on the news and hear something bad about the Middle-East and, of course, that would create a negative image in their mind that could make them prejudge me as a person, or at least that was one of my guesses as to why I got rejected so often.

It wasn't easy to remain positive, but I was trying not to let anything take the hope away from me: the hope that one day I would find her. I was trying to find my only love even more proactively and more consciously than before. Over time, I had been able to further deepen and purify my understanding of love. All these failures had helped to immensely develop my understanding of what love is and what isn't.

I was becoming more convinced that the way people initially select their partners is the root of most problems they encounter later on. In other words, I had come to believe that relationship problems are first and foremost due to mindsets and then only secondly due to lack of relationship techniques or communication skills. After talking to Justin, I had realized that a lot of people based their relationships on sparks, meaning that they would not consider anyone unless they had a crush on them—or at least a spark.

As time was passing, more students were joining the Egoless Love Club. As I was getting to know them, I was realizing that some of them were getting involved for many reasons other than believing in true love. But I kept the club open to anyone who would like to participate, or even to help with the logistics of it. Thanks to those people who were willing to help, it was now possible to accomplish a task I had always wanting to do—that is, to conduct a statistical study on how people actually think about love. After all, I was a geek! So I used the help of new club members to gather some data on what percentage of students have similar styles of thinking when it comes to love. So we prepared almost a hundred questionnaire forms and every one of us tried to find other students who would respond to these questions with their most honest answers. I wanted to learn how many of us approach love with a spark, exchange, fear, or egoless mindsets.

We made a rule that each of us is only allowed to ask these questions from people of the same sex. I wanted to avoid any social pressure effects on the responses. Not surprisingly though, when asked questions about meaning of love by a person of the same sex, boys tended to resist answering very clearly while girls in general had more affinity towards sharing their ideas more openly, but all in all, I hoped to get more honest responses this way.

It appeared that more than fifty-three percent of males and about eight percent of girls agreed to some extent with the basic ideas of the exchange mindset. It showed itself in many different shapes and forms, many different words and phrases, but all things considered, the underlying principle was the same. The members of this group believed that a relationship was not really about love but it was about satisfying needs. In other words, their mindset was that in relationships, you want certain things and you give certain things in return, simply an exchange or barter in its core! One popular idea among people who believed in the exchange mindset was the notion that guys only want sex and girls want relationships and romance. Some girls of this group considered falling in love with any guy equivalent to letting your heart be broken sooner or later, which was also a sign of the fear mindset to me.

The most common mentality towards love among the students was the spark mindset. It turned out that eighty-six percent of girls and sixty-four percent of guys defined love as that moment of excitement and that special feeling of adoring someone. In other words, liking someone or something intensely—the same concept that Justin called a love spark. They believed that without an initial spark, love could never form; they believed you could be friends without any initial sparks, but surely not in love. They defined love as being passionate about something, such as a car, a career, or about someone—a girl, a boy, or both. This definition of love surprised me.; when I define true love as an egoless and unselfish deep feeling towards your one and only love, how can that one and only be a car?!

The data showed that most people, statistically speaking, have a mix of several or all mindsets when it comes to love, but for the majority, there was one prominent mindset ruling their lives and behaviors. That is, many people—at the same time—believed in some form of the exchange mindset and some form of the spark mindset.

The variation in responses and beliefs was perhaps as high as the number of students who responded. Quite often, the students we asked weren't conscious about what they truly believed in and needed to be pushed a bit to do some soul searching. But despite all the different words and phrases used, the underlying principles governing the most common belief system about love was the love spark mentality and then after that, the exchange mindset. The mindsets of fear and egoless love were the least mentioned, respectively. The spark mindset was more common among female students and that of exchange was more common among male students.

Back in school, things were gradually getting back to

normal. As the news about the drug overdose was gradually forgotten, the school executives were relieved of the public relations nightmare they had been dealing with, so they were once again letting the college kids enjoy a little weed smoking fun. Yet things weren't exactly like before. Justin was the only one who used to throw parties off-campus and with him going away, all the big parties were the boring ones regulated by the university.

Justin was very much missed by a lot of students who loved his crazy parties, but there was no way the university would accept him again. I heard from one of his close friends that he had moved back to Dallas, his hometown, so he wasn't planning to show up, or so I thought.

One night when I was sitting at a desk in the common room of the student center, doing some administrative stuff for the budget of the club, my phone rang. It was Justin! He said he was back in town because he wanted to see me; he said there was something very important that he wanted to talk to me about. He said he really would appreciate if I could make it. It seemed like he was pretty anxious, so after some hesitation, I accepted.

We met the next day in a café off-campus. He seemed very calm this time and politer than before. After we ordered our drinks and sat down at a table, he abruptly started the conversation, "Thanks for showing up today. I know I was a douche to you that night and I'm sorry for that, dude."

I answered, "No worries. Very frankly, I didn't really get offended by your vulgar language, but the content was offensive. Later on, I realized a lot of people actually do choose their love partner based on the shallow mentalities you talked about that night, so it's not only you. You just spoke of them out loud and bluntly in a way others may not. Anyway, I heard the news about your dismissal from the school. I hope you are okay."

He said, "Thanks, but I couldn't care less about being dismissed from the university."

From the type of lifestyle he was famous for, I wasn't

particularly shocked by his answer. But still, you would think he should be upset even just a little bit. I said, "So you are not upset about being forced out of school? Even a bit?"

He said, "Nope! I wasn't in the right place anyway. Actually, I wanted to talk to you about that. After they threw me out, I had some time to think about what was going on with my life. The overdose incident reminded me of something; something I had purposefully forgotten for a long time."

Well, that was surprising! A party-animal like Justin had self-reflected?! I mean, Justin was praised as the god of shallow pleasures among his friends. Frankly, deep thoughts, inner reflections, and emotional awakenings weren't exactly what I expected to hear from him. I couldn't hide my surprise when I said, "Oh wow! Are you really okay, Justin?"

He laughed and said, "I know it's not something you'd expect to hear from me, but let me back up and explain how I became the Justin you knew. Since I was a kid, I always questioned why things exist the way they do. It's funny, I remember asking my dad questions that were totally bizarre for a kid to ask. One time, I asked my dad why we live and stones don't. Of course, he had no idea how to answer that. Eventually, these existential questions seriously started weighing on me, especially as a teenager. I wanted to know why we exist, or what is our purpose in life. For a long time, I tried to stick to religion and God. I was hoping religion could give me some ultimate meaning in life. As a person who was born into a hardcore Evangelic Baptist family, I used to go to church every Sunday, constantly trying to convert other people by inviting them to my church. I prayed a lot too—I pretty much had this constant internal conversation with God. But the more I tried to have faith in religion, the more I realized there was nothing special about it. At first, I started to doubt the hateful position my church was taking against homosexuals, condemning them to hell! I have always been a straight man myself, but judging gay people like that didn't sit right with me, you know? I tried to talk to all sorts of religious role-models I had, but no response could rationalize the extreme intolerance and hatred that my church was showing towards the LGBTQ community. Soon after, I started to doubt the Bible, and eventually, I stopped believing in the existence of any god. Religion gradually seemed to me to be just an organized scam instead of the holy source of meaning I was seeking in life. Then, I tried lots of different lifestyles in the hope that at least one of them would give me a sense of purpose. I tried everything from Buddhism to Satanism. Nothing! Nothing was able to give my life any deep and sacred meaning. Nothing meant anything anymore. All I could see was emptiness. Following came a period of pretty severe depression.

My dad hired a famous psychologist and paid him loads of money to visit me at home. He gradually convinced me that my own happiness is the only reason for living. He convinced me that what mattered was my own happiness and whatever makes me happy is and should be the meaning of my life. This was a bit unsatisfactory at first, but the more I stopped caring about finding some higher purpose, the happier I got. Nothing had any meaning and I was okay with it! Fun and pleasure were the new gods for me. My dad had enough money to pay for anything I wanted. I lost myself in pleasure and fun. After all, this was everyone's dream life and I was living their dream, and the best part was I didn't have to go through any of the hassles that ordinary people might have to go through to get that kind of life. When I started college, that lifestyle reached a whole new level. I didn't have to live with my extremely religious parents anymore, so there was no need to hide what I did! I drowned myself in alcohol, drugs, and casual sex. This all was a token of worship to this new god: the god of pleasure, fun, and self-love. It made me calm. It made me not need any meaning in life anymore. It made me feel okay about not having some higher purpose, and this was the case until I met you. You made me question that lifestyle."

I shockingly asked, "Me? What do you mean?"

He answered, "Yeah, I saw you trying anything you possibly could to make true love happen in your life—a sacred concept I had never seen anyone else believe in so deeply. That night we talked, I wasn't trying to be an asshole to you. My heart was touched by the innocent idea of true love you were living for, and that made me defensive to protect my ideology of pleasure and instant gratification. Thanks to all the parties I've hosted, I've met many girls and boys in my life, and let me tell you: for the most part, people are shallow, man. You, on the other hand, seem to be fighting for something in your life, and that's what I've always been looking for—something sacred that's worth fighting for."

"Believe it or not, I regret how I acted that night more than I regret being dismissed from the university. When you left, something in me woke up: that old need for a truly sacred meaning in life. For a long time, I had lied to myself. I had convinced myself that such meaning does not exist and so, I only tried to have fun and please myself. But that night, the more I thought about what you were doing, the more curious I became about your ideas."

"I don't really know much about what you call true love, but what I can easily see is that true love is adding a shit-load of sacred meaning to your life, and that's what I have always been thirsty for. So dude, I am sorry for my aggressive behavior, and I understand if you hate me enough not to want to share your ideas anymore, but if you do, that would mean a lot to me. I really want to know more about this true love you talk about."

Wow! I could not believe this. Was this really Justin? Sitting right in front of me, asking me to explain more about true love? The same Justin who thought love is a myth?! The same Justin who believed being a playboy is what smart guys do and the rest are just losers?!

I could not believe the scene I was seeing in front of me. But at the same time, I had never seen anyone so passionate about hearing what I had to say about true love. He had a keen and humble motivation to know more, and the source of that motivation was a deep internal need for meaning.

I had some mixed feelings about how to proceed. I could not believe he was actually respecting my views now, but at the same time, he seemed very sincere this time.

So I said, "Wow! I'm honestly a bit shocked at how you transformed over this short time. I mean you criticized the whole thing in an almost cruel manner and now you are asking to know more? But I guess I'm happy you did change. Anyway, what do you want to know?"

He said, "You are right, buddy. I was pretty cruel to you the other night and I'm really sorry for that. I was trying to neglect a part of my soul by heavy drinking, drugs, and chicks, but you helped me realize there might still be hope for me to find a meaning that's worth living for. That's why I want to know more about your ideas on true love. What is this true love? How does it differ from the regular love that breaks hearts almost every time?"

No doubt, he seemed sincere and thirsty to learn about true love and this was very precious to me. It was amazing that he showed so much courage to get out of his comfort zone, traveled all the way from Dallas, and asked to learn more about true love.

I had a sip of the hot chocolate I had ordered and said, "The past is past; Justin, I don't care anymore what you told me that night. I am so very happy to hear your genuine interest in learning about true love. Before I say anything, though, I want to confess something. In these six months after the night we talked, I conducted a survey about love among students. Surprisingly, you were right about the reality of how most people perceive love. I am sure a high percentage of people have good intentions, but it is unfortunate to see how widespread the selfish mindsets are. People know that this same old method they fall in love often brings nothing but a broken heart, but they still fall in love the same way because maybe they don't know any better."

"You enlightened me that night about spark and exchange mindsets. How some people seek relationships only for the benefits the other person offers, or how people think love is when they adore someone, when that person makes them feel waves of affection, or when that other person is exactly the type they want. True love, though, is not just a need or a feeling, but a lifestyle; it's a commitment to the sacredness of the love, to serve your beloved with all you are. For true lovers, the ultimate happiness is bringing a smile on the lips of their beloved."

"You know? I am sure many people have the mindset of egoless love hidden somewhere in their hearts. Perhaps some people experience it in their lives to some extent or for some period of time. We are all humans and in spite of our differences, we all share the same core. True lovers are human too; they have feelings just like any other human, but they don't base their relationships only on shallow sparks. They have needs like anyone else, but they never allow themselves to fake love or think of love as an exchange; instead, true lovers always seek ways to selflessly make their beloved happy, even if that means difficulty for themselves.

You asked what true love is, Justin. It's tough, but I'll try my best to put it in words. True love is when you commit yourself to selflessly put your beloved first, always. It is important to understand that true love is a lifestyle, not just a feeling; it could even start before you meet that special significant other. True love is a mindset, a mentality that is distinctly different from falling in love with a mindset of exchange or the spark mentality."

I continued, "Does that make any sense, Justin?"

He nodded his head and said, "Yeah, it makes sense, but how is this mindset of true love different from the usual ways people fall in love? Like could you explain more how the mentality of true love is different from mentality of love spark or exchange? What is it about this egoless true love that makes you go through all of this effort?"

I felt the conversation was going in the right direction. I had finally found someone who showed some genuine interest towards understanding the mindset of egoless true love. This was such a precious moment, and I had to do my best to do justice to the beauty of true love, so I said, "The differences are absolutely immense! The most important aspect of true love is its selflessness. We all have egos and we all like ourselves better than others. That's not a bad thing, except no relationship lasts unless both parties start to be selfless. The magic ingredient of any beautiful true love is the selflessness that the true lovers develop individually and then offer to each other. This selflessness, if deep enough, gives birth to a lot of lovely things like honesty, kindness, compassion, patience, absolute loyalty, and many more. It is often not the other way around."

"If two people are truly in love, each of them loves the other even more than themselves. There is nothing in the world true lovers won't do for their beloved. Their beloved's happiness is a million times better than their own, if they had to choose only one. The slightest light of joy in their beloved's eyes makes the true lovers' hearts burst. As such, their beloved's sadness is the heaviest burden on their shoulder. True lovers never get tired of love. True love never ends."

"Should true lovers happen to disagree on something, they would discuss it, but neither of them would try to win over the other person! Above all, true lovers are to make sacrifices for the sake of love. For true lovers, nothing in the world, even life itself, is nearly as precious as each other."

"True love is not a spark, but It's a divine and eternal light! The secret to true love is that for a true lover, love has always been the most important thing in life and therefore, the true lover has practiced an egoless mindset for a long time before even meeting the beloved. This practice of selflessness makes love an essential part of true lovers' soul and persona. This is the key!"

"Now let me compare this selfless true love with the love spark or exchange mindsets. No one in their right mind can deny that a spark is beautiful and even powerful. The way our stomach sinks and it feels like the person you have a crush on is the cutest, the most beautiful, and the kindest human being; the way it makes us not see the bad parts of the beloved and be drawn to their good parts."

"But all I'm saying about the spark is that it is a sign you like someone but sparks by no means are a sign of selfless true love. Sometimes we are self-aware of the shallow qualities we base our relationships upon, and sometimes not. Some people equate the spark to love, but the person who gives you the sparks may not necessarily be a true lover. Liking someone very much is not equal as loving them, as simple as that! Usually our imagination builds upon the sparks, and exaggerates the good qualities of the person we feel a spark for. If you are in a relationship with a person you have a crush on, it could feel awesome. You could feel so good about yourself and your life, but all of that is because you mistakenly think this spark is the same as true love—but it isn't, and people realize that when it burns out!"

Justin abruptly interrupted me and asked with a confused face, "So, just checking to see if I got it right: Are you saying you don't need to be attracted to a person to fall in true love with them?"

I smiled because it was actually a very good question. I said, "No, that's not at all what I believe. In fact, except occasionally, I don't think it is a good idea to start a relationship with someone you have absolutely no potential to form a physical attraction to. What I mean is that true lovers don't need to date the hottest people they can find; they give those who don't immediately give them sparks a chance to get to know them. Who knows? There are people out there who are not necessarily the best-looking, but they might have the most profound capacity for true love in their hearts. True lovers look for true love in the heart of people when they date. People of the love spark mentality, as you know, believe that they must feel warm and fuzzy towards a person before even considering dating them. As such, a very common notion among people who find their beloved through the spark mindset is that love is when you like someone very much, and so when they feel extreme passion towards someone, they think they have found true love; not knowing that true love has nothing to do with presence or absence of that initial spark."

Now another common mindset is that of exchange. Some

people look for certain materialistic benefits or certain ways they want to be treated. If someone provides them that comfortable and ideal life they want, they fall for that person. I'm not only talking about gold-diggers. The exchange mentality could be any thought that seems like barter in a relationship. It could look normal externally, but I'm talking about intentions when I talk about mindsets. To the people who have based their relationships on exchange mindset, a girlfriend, a boyfriend, a husband, or a wife is just like a car, a house, a piece of land, or even a pair of shoes—that is, a replaceable necessity to have in life. They try to find a man or a woman with the best options. To these people, true love is never needed: you can be in a romantic relationship with someone without any true love. They get married to make their life more comfortable, or to have children, or even to lower their tax bracket! They get married to the best candidate they can find, in order to avoid being alone or to have someone to have sex with, and to enjoy other benefits they may get from a relationship or marriage. The people with such a mentality often try to give the least and get the most out of any relationship."

I took another sip of the hot chocolate, which was now cold chocolate, since our conversation had taken a while, but I was having the most enjoyable time: explaining how the mindset of true egoless love can solve many people's romantic problems.

Justin was looking at me with his right hand underneath his chin. He had a very thoughtful expression on his face. It looked like his mind was processing a lot of information, which was a great sign! I wanted to do my best to help him understand the point, so I rapidly made up an example and said, "I just thought of a little story to illustrate what I mean. The story starts with four friends who go to the same high school. Their names are Mr. Sparky, Mr. Trader, Mr. Fearful, and Mr. Lover. These four friends have four different mindsets towards love, which shapes four completely different paths in life for each of them. Mr. Sparky happens to be exclusively following the mindset of love spark. Mr. Trader is, on the other hand, following the mindset of exchange. Mr. Fearful is in a relationship to cover his fears, and obviously, Mr. Lover is following the mindset of egoless love, so needless to say, Mr. Lover is my favorite of the bunch. Now, like I said before, I believe all people naturally have a mix of all of these mindsets, not just one, but what matters is which one they live by. What matters is which one of these mindsets our romantic decisions are based upon. Anyway, Let's see how these four imaginary characters in my little story think in different stages of their romantic lives. Are you ready?"

"Sure, dude," he said while scratching his head.

I smiled and continued, "Awesome! Okay then, let's start the story from the time they are all teenagers, young and full of energy, and of course, testosterone!"

He laughed.

I continued, "To Mr. Sparky and Mr. Trader, life was all about discovering and pleasure. They bragged to each other about the quantity and quality of the girls they had slept with at that early age. Mr. Sparky was a hot-looking football player on the high school team. High school girls literally fought each other to get his attention. He used this opportunity with pride to get as much sex as possible with the hottest girls in school. Mr. Trader wasn't as hot, but knew how to get what he wanted. Mr. Fearful was also in a relationship, but not because he liked that girl; only because he was afraid how others might make fun of him if he remained a virgin. As for Mr. Lover, the seed of true love had started to take root in his young heart. He had realized that true love was selfless. This selfless true love made him to be a deeper person, compared to his friends of the same age. This true love made him treat everyone and everything with a sense of kindness and respect. He was good to his parents, to his neighbors, to animals, and everyone liked him. Every day, he practiced being considerate, kind, caring, patient, and understanding.

Now a few years passed and all four guys in this little story were now thinking about finding a serious relationship, but for different reasons. Mr. Trader had been faking romantic relationships in the past just to benefit from the sex, but then he started to feel like he wanted more than sex; he wanted to have children of his own someday and without a wife, he couldn't have any. One day, he contemplated exactly what he wanted in life and then listed the qualities that he wanted in a girl—all the qualities that he thought would make him happy. For instance, he only accepted girls who were hotter than 6. He and his friends had created this made-up scale by which they evaluated how attractive girls were, a scale of 1 to 10 with number ten being the hottest. Another quality he was looking for was that his girl should be very much interested in watching national baseball, especially his favorite team. He wanted a girl who was into playing video games with him or at least would have no problem if he spent his leisure time playing video games. He wanted his girl to be at least college educated. He also only considered girls who believed in his religion because his religion played an important role in his family. Basically, his perspective towards love was similar to ordering a dish at a restaurant. So, Mr. Trader started a relationship with this hot girl from his church that seemed to share a lot of his interests and they both seemed to enjoy each other's company. He was not sure if he would have any future with that girl or not, but he didn't care as long as he was happy with the benefits. To him, love was not required to start a relationship because any relationship would give him some experience he could use in life. If it didn't work or if he got tired of this girl, he could always dump her and move on to another. For him, a girlfriend had always been something you just had to have; just like a car in a city without good public transportation, it just makes life easier. Mr. Sparky, however, had a lot of sexual experiences of all kinds by now, but none of them felt like the one that was meant to be. There were some girls who were interested in him, but he never gave them any chance no matter how interested they were, simply because they weren't hot enough for him and he wasn't feeling that spark he should have felt. But a year ago in college, he met this very special girl that he really liked a lot, and she liked him too. They had been dating for about a year. He felt like there was something so special about her that made him go crazy. She told him she felt the same way about him too. They called this feeling love. They were very happy and were having really good times together. Mr. Fearful got married to the same high school girlfriend he didn't really like because he was scared if he let go of her and searched for love, he might never find another girl, so he held on to what he had. As for Mr. Lover, he had not yet had any relationships. He didn't want to start relationships just for the sake of being in one, and he had not been lucky enough yet to find a girl who would understand and appreciate the true love he had been cultivating. He had all the hopes in the world, though, that one day he would find his one and only love. He had been preparing himself for that time. Mr. Lover remained social. He kept his eyes open and remained optimistic that one day he would find the love of his life. He wanted to try any method to get in contact with more people; he had even joined some online dating services.

"A few more years passed. Mr. Trader got married to his girlfriend from church who shared a lot of his hobbies and interests. They both enjoyed very similar hobbies like playing video games and watching baseball; they both wanted a big religious family with a few children; they both belonged to the same church. His thought was if he married a girl who was very similar to him and wanted the same things in life, then the gain would be worth the pain. He believed the most important disadvantage of marriage might be losing his freedom, so overall, he felt he was gaining more than he was losing by marrying a pretty girl who also enjoyed and wanted similar things in life. Mr. Trader liked his wife very much. The first six months of their marriage was as good as the time they were dating. He tried to do things that his wife liked in order to keep her happy. You know? He really believed in the expression, "happy wife, happy life!" Mr. Sparky got married to his girlfriend too. With every new date they went on, he felt a stronger spark towards his girlfriend, a kind of spark and passion they would watch in romantic Hollywood movies. Mr. Sparky's rationale for marrying his girlfriend was that, based on their relationship thus far, he believed the passion would continue to grow and he would love her even when they got old and rusty. In fact, Mr. Sparky and his wife too were extremely happy together during the first year of their marriage. As for Mr. Lover, he had not yet found his true love, but he didn't see this as a competition. He didn't believe there was a set time for finding his love; rather, he focused on improving himself so he would deserve that love when he found it. He was looking for someone who could understand his selfless type of love, someone who would fully appreciate how different his true love was from the spark or exchange mindsets. He was waiting to find someone who firmly believed in egoless love; someone who appreciated his selflessness and in turn would make the effort to love him as well in his good and bad, sweet and sour, rich and poor. Even though Mr. Lover didn't come from a hardcore religious background, he always believed in one sentence of the Bible: that man and wife become one. He knew the exact meaning of this Bible verse in his bones. He knew two true lovers could form a unified soul through the sacrifices they made, and as such, he was satisfied with nothing else but a true egoless love. Mr. Lover's friends and family put a lot of pressure on him, whether knowingly or unknowingly, to make him get married as soon as possible. Very regularly, Mr. Lover was asked if he had found anyone yet. But he never wanted to rush it. Over time, his true love became purer. He was more prepared than ever to truly, genuinely, and consistently offer his love to his beloved when he did find her."

"A few more years passed. Mr. Trader was already the father of two cute little kids and his wife was pregnant with the third one. Mr. Trader was not taking care of himself much anymore, nor was he taking good care of his wife's emotions. He had stopped celebrating their anniversary, stopped buying her flowers, and stopped trying to do anything to make his wife happy. Sometimes he would do nice stuff, but only as an empty gesture. He and his wife had both been working a lot and when they got home, they just preferred to watch TV and go to bed; they didn't have any time for each other anymore, or perhaps that was the best excuse they could find. Mr. Trader always complained about the married life to his colleagues at work and told them it was not worth it. He missed all the casual sex he had when he was younger and now with these damn children he hardly ever had any sex with his wife. His marriage felt like a chain fastened to his legs, taking his freedom away from him but not adding the benefits he thought it would. He was tired of being responsible for other people! He was responsible as a dad, as a husband, as an employee, but what did he get in return? He would never help wash the dishes or clean the house or anything else unless his wife made him, because why should he want more work for himself? When their one-year-old screamed in the other room in the middle of the night, he would never volunteer; instead, he would let his wife's sleep be interrupted rather than his own. He was just trying to hang in there by fulfilling the minimum responsibilities possible. His wife had been wondering for a long time what happened to the amazing romance they once had. As for Mr. Sparky, the spark had magically gone away the same way it magically appeared. After the first few years they spent married, Mr. Sparky and his wife got really used to seeing each other. The magic feeling was no longer ruling their relationship. What had replaced the spark were their egos, just like in the case of Mr. Trader's life. For a long time, they thought they could reclaim the spark by adding some spice to their life. They tried every technique out there, but excitement fled from their life the way cash was fleeing from their bank account. One day when Mr. Sparky was sitting alone in a bar after work, a very beautiful girl sat on the next seat to him and started the conversation with him. He suddenly realized he still had all the charm and manly attractiveness that had made high school girls fight over him back in the day. Their conversation went so naturally and smooth and it lasted for a couple of hours. Mr. Sparky knew his wife was waiting for him at home and it was probably a bad idea to continue drinking with this attractive girl, but this girl was rekindling the lost spark he felt years ago. He couldn't understand it, but there was something about this new girl that made him want her so badly. It was the same spark, but with a different girl. Anyway, one thing led to another, he went home with her, and they had sex. He left that girl's place the same night in a miserable walk of shame, but when his wife didn't question him for being late, he didn't feel so bad anymore about what happened. He wondered in his head, 'Shouldn't my own happiness be the most important thing in my life?'"

"He continued the rationalization in his head, 'If I feel good with other girls, why on the earth should I be ashamed of it? Why should I stand my wife just because I once fell in love with her back in the day? I don't feel the love anymore, so why not let her go?'"

"Soon, he had completely rationalized cheating on his wife by telling himself that accidents happen! He realized that he could recapture the same lost spark every now and then, as long as he did not let his wife find out about it."

"Mr. Fearful's married life wasn't any better than the other two, but he was sticking it out. Even though he was not at all happy in his married life, he could not even think of getting a divorce because he was afraid of all the financial and emotional consequences a divorce might bring."

"As for Mr. Lover, he had finally found his one and only. He and his girl had their differences in personality, character, and even life goals, but they both shared the sacred eternal light of true love in their hearts! She knew very well that a selfless true lover who would sacrifice anything for her was the only one who deserved her, and she truly appreciated that quality in Mr. Lover. With every breath he took in, Mr. Lover loved this girl more and promised himself to never let her go. The purified true love they both had been practicing all their lives was paying off. They were both committed to always putting each other first. They were both ready to protect each other in hard times, even if it meant a lot of sacrifices and compromises. They both knew that the most important thing in their lives was each other, and with this true love, they began their holy marriage. They spoke the vows to always love each other from the sincerest part of their hearts and they knew this would be a life journey together."

"Life went on and a few more years passed. Mr. Trader and his wife had gotten divorced with four children. They just realized they had changed so much in time and they did not want the same things they once wanted. Their three girls had to live with their mom and the boy had to live with his dad. Their children did not get the benefits of a healthy family. They had to choose between living with their dad or mom, and this was difficult. Mr. Sparky and his wife had gotten divorced too. That one cheating incident led Mr. Sparky to cheat many more times and Mrs. Sparky finally found out about them. After the divorce, Mr. Sparky continued to seek casual sex with other girls. He was hot and he had no problem making some shallow girls fall for him. But he was the same person and he treated those new girls the same way he treated his first wife—by cheating on them. However, Mr. Lover and his wife went through all the best and worst of life together. Mr. Lover never ever let himself even think about betraying his beloved because his commitment to true love always made him put her first over his will, instinct, and needs. They were both getting older together and, of course, their beauty and youth were fading, but their love was growing because they had not based their relationship on any sparks in the first place. They had based their love and marriage on true love, which meant that they still loved each other just like the first day they met, even after all the beauty and attraction had gone away. They had their differences, but every time they disagreed on something, they tried their best to find a solution that both were happy with and the key to that was their selflessness, which enabled them to compromise gladly for the good of both of them. The mutual true love between Mr. Lover and his wife was real, consistent, and truly beautiful. Mr. Lover always kept reminding his wife in some way that he would love her forever. His wife also always appreciated his true love and responded to it. The couple was raising two beautiful children and kept providing them with love and all the tools they needed for success. When their children were little and needed attention day and night, Mr. Lover always volunteered to wake up whenever the babies started crying; he preferred his own sleep to be interrupted rather than his wife's. When his wife saw this repeatedly happening, she didn't let him wake up all the time, but sometimes let him sleep and tiptoed to children's room so as not to wake him up. Selfless love existed mutually between them; the selfless love in which each spouse equated the happiness and comfort of the other one with their own, so there was no battle over power. Mr. Lover was as good of a father as he was a lover; he was always there for his family whether financially, mentally, or emotionally. Mr. Lover and his wife had become closer to each other through the difficulties of life."

"Now my brother Justin, I made up this little story on the spot just to try to answer your question about how true love is different from the kind of love that is based on the sparks, fear, or exchange mindsets. There are many ways true love is very different, but if I have to describe the difference in only one word, I would say the heart of true love is selflessness; it is a lifelong commitment to the internal promise you make to the essence of true love itself to put your beloved, always, the same as your own self. This selflessness does not mean a lack of self-confidence, but it means you become one with your love. Every other aspect of true love is rooted in this core concept of selflessness. True lovers are honest in their love, they are genuine, they are kind, they are humble, they are caring of their beloved, they listen to what the beloved says and wants, they try their best to understand their beloved, but the very core of all of these is that internal sacred light of egoless true love."

"So you told me about your thirst for a deep meaning in life, Justin. It may interest you, my friend, that as a result of a lifelong practice of true love, the true lovers discover a sacred meaning in standing up for love. I want you to know that what I tell you about true love is not a fictional story; its potential exists somewhere in the heart of each and every human being. True love is no fairy tale! True lovers find that sacred meaning in their hearts and then never let it go. I know for a fact that all I tell you is alive in my own heart and actions, so I am a tiny testimony to that!"

There were a few seconds of silence between us. Justin was staring out the window near our table; his eyes were tied to a tree across from the street outside the café. He seemed to be in a deep internal conversation with himself. I did not want to interrupt his train of thought, so I remained silent and gave him a couple of minutes, until he turned his head towards me and asked, "Dude, I think I get it now! I know many people choose to find relationships based on sparks because they are looking for instant gratification of their own desires, and they think this will make them happy, but you say true love is different. In true love, the lovers are trying to be all giving to their partners even though they might go through a lot of hard times. The true lovers put the happiness of their partner above their own because they're unified by their love. Am I right?"

I was so happy that I was able to communicate the idea of true love to him, so I smiled and said, "Yup! You got it!"

He said, "There is another thing, dude! I don't mean to be rude again, but do you remember what I told you that night? I apologize for the words I used, but I still think there aren't many people out there who want to find their partners based on the selfless type of love you talk about. I mean, for so long, you have been wholeheartedly searching for that love of your life and we both know you haven't found it, so what do you think the reason is? Isn't it that no one even remotely wants to understand or follow these really deep thoughts? I'm just being honest."

I said, "You know, Justin, you may be right. There may not be so many people out there who truly understand or appreciate the kind of true love I've been talking about. There are some people who can't even imagine why they would put anyone before themselves. There are also many people out there in this world who completely understand what I talk about, but they still prefer the fantasies of sparks or ease of exchange mindsets. But the truth, my friend, is that a true lover seeks true love even if the whole world is against it. True lovers are in love with love itself."

He said, "I'm confused, so you don't care if you don't find anyone?"

I said, "Of course I do. All I want in life is to be a good lover to that one and only love of my life."

He said, "Man, now I'm officially confused. So you agree that many girls may prefer a handsome, charming, but selfish guy over your entire kind, honest, and selfless true love. At the same time, you really want to find a girl. Then how can you still want to stick to this true love?! You even know this makes your life very tough, but you still want to follow true love? Dude, isn't it easier to just give up on true love and enjoy life with whoever you find based on shallow sparks just like other people do?"

He was almost repeating the same ideology as that night only with different words, but I felt this time was different. It seemed he genuinely wanted to understand true love better this time and even that question was more to understand my persistence on true love rather than encouraging me to be a player. So I answered, "Let me put it this way: I don't want my future wife to be in love with me for how I look, because what if I lose all the charm and beauty in an accident or something? Will she love me then too? I don't want her to love me for the strong muscles and the abs because what if I get disfigured in an accident or somehow lose all that physical strength? Or when I get old and nasty; will she still love me then too? I don't want her to love me for how rich I may be or the good life I may be providing her because what if I lose it all in a wrong investment or something? Will she still love me when I'm weak and broke? I don't want a woman to love me for the things I do or even shallow things we have in common because desires and feelings change over time. Will she still love me when we may not have so much in common anymore?"

"The mentality of a true lover is based on appreciation of

true love itself. It is very important that true lovers understand and accept all the differences they have with their beloved. True lovers even sincerely help their beloved to achieve those different goals; goals that they might not personally relate with. True lover couples help each other rise again with the power of love if they are ever financially broken. True lover couples love each other even when they get old and their skin wrinkles and their muscles get weak. When they change over time, they find new things together. True lovers, my friend, are part of one unified soul! If one doesn't function, the other won't just leave, but will do everything to restore it, even if the path to do so may go through hell. I'm not talking about one month or two, I'm not even talking about years, I'm talking about forever. You know why they can love for such long periods and not get bored of each other? Because they did not select each other based on any shallow sparks or benefits, but they selected each other out of mutual egoless love that gave them courage and appreciation to always stand up for each other. The sparks and benefits of the marriage were just added bonuses, but their relationship is based on egoless love, and all the other things will follow."

"Now let me clarify two things: First, like I said before, the healthy true love is always two-sided. If one half of a relationship is a selfless true lover and the other is a self-centered egocentric maniac, I would never recommend that lover to continue that relationship. In fact, I would highly encourage selfless true lovers to find other egoless true lovers. It is heart-breaking to see a true lover is living with a selfish partner."

"Second, I'm not saying true lovers don't need some physical attraction to fall in love, but I do say true lovers know that what really matters above all is sacred selflessness in love. Selflessness is not something that will be created when you are together. Sparks can't create selfless love. Both the man and the woman should have already prepared themselves over time to be truly selfless. Of course, true lovers select partners to whom they feel some level of attraction, but the true lovers don't ever make that spark a necessity; instead they try to find someone who understands love and then they let the spark gradually develop. They select someone who loves them for who they are inside rather than how they look or what they do. True lovers sincerely offer to their partner their entire soul and them being hot or not does not change that. This is a very delicate subject; I hope it makes sense."

His eyes flicked from me towards the window again as if he had a personal memory he was afraid to share. Then he rapidly changed the subject and said, "Anyway dude, you might be right about everything, I don't know. Sparks are so huge among people of this day and time that it feels like no one ever chooses the way you preach. By the way, why do think that is? I mean why do think so many people like to find relationships based on emotional sparks, or even the pros and cons of a relationship, but not on selfless love?"

As we were having this conversation, it was becoming progressively more clear to me that Justin was indeed a smart kid, despite the fact that based on our previous talk, his choice of words and his dirty mind needed a bit of polish. This thought brought another smile to my face and while I was scratching my head, I said, "That's another great question honestly, but again, very difficult to answer. Well, I have a strong belief that at least the majority of people, if not all, know the need for an egoless love somewhere deep in their hearts, but in many cases, they mix this sacred feeling with other desires, passions, or fantasies they have. Sometimes, they simply don't know how to transform that internal thirst for true love into a reality in the external world."

"Another huge factor is the media. People of this day and age often tend to form strong and usually unconscious beliefs based on what they see or hear in the media. It's just amazing how common it is for people to get their information from TV, movies, music, and social media. The media is a tool, and of course, it becomes as good as what the policy makers and media gurus make it to be. Media, these days, does an absolutely phenomenal job in promoting sparks and sex. There isn't a single day that I don't see examples of it around me. For instance, how popular is a romance movie where two normal-looking people fall in love in a very boring but realistic way? In most of these romantic movies, the actor and actress who are supposed to fall in love are so carefully handpicked to be the most gorgeous actors possible! Why? They admit it's only because it sells in the box office. Now, the young person who watches the romantic Hollywood movies deeply wishes to have someone very handsome and gorgeous for him or herself too; no normal-looking human would be satisfying anymore. These stories and movies bombard us from the time we are little children, depicting a charming prince who comes to save a gorgeous princess. When we grow up, we forget that the sacrifices a lover makes is the point of those stories, not the shimmering luxury of a royal life. Or think about the fact that thousands of girls and boys might have a crush on a particular singer, actor, actress, or sport player while a normal looking true lover might just never be good enough for these folks! In fact, not only does the media form a considerable amount of people's physical, sexual, and emotional preferences, but it also significantly manipulates people's conceptions of what love even is."

"Another cultural factor behind the widespread existence of spark and exchange mindsets is individualism. People, especially in west, are encouraged to think that whatever their heart desires or whatever their mind believes is absolutely the right thing, though in reality, we humans can be very much deceived by our own feelings. You know? Individualism, if used in the proper ways, is actually a great thing. Scores of inventors are pioneers of their fields because they respected their individuality, which allowed them to insist on their own radical and innovative ideas. But individualism must not be followed in each and every single aspect of our lives, especially not in our romantic lives. Unfortunately, individualistic concepts often lead to pure selfishness if exercised in improper occasions. Selfish people cannot be true lovers even if they give you the warmest and fuzziest spark of all time. A selfish person who loves you because of a spark might act selfless for some time, but after the spark and attraction goes away and real hardships of living comes along, that's when the truth is revealed. That is, the selfish person will return to his or her selfish nature. The point is that the number of people who select their partners based on true love is extremely low in today's world, and it is diminishing as we speak. I started a club called the Egoless Love Club, as an effort to keep the true love alive so that the next generations won't think true love is just something you can find only in fiction. I want true love to be a visible, factual element of our society, live and dynamic. I want to pursue this cause by informing people about true love and how different it is from spark, fear, and exchange mindsets."

He said, "Yo, man, I get it! What you say makes sense to me, but I can't feel it in my heart like you do! They say, 'once a player, always a player!' Maybe I'll never be a true lover. Maybe it's just not for me. I don't know. But what I do know is I really admire your commitment to it. I can imagine it gives you a strong sense of purpose, doesn't it?"

I said, "My friend, it takes time. Don't rush it. I very sincerely believe the sacred mentality of egoless true love is in the heart of every human being, only some of us awaken it over time. I suggest you take your time and think about it. Over time, I hope that this continuous mental digestion will awaken the sacred source of true love energy in your heart. The energy that makes you a chevalier for your beloved; the energy that makes you want to fight for her, stand by her, and even selflessly die for her."

He said, "Yeah, I'll think about what you said. I promise!" and that was the end of our conversation about true love. After a little bit of chatting, we said goodbye and left the café.

A couple of months passed after my rather extensive conversation with Justin, but I did not hear from him. Honestly, I was a little disappointed, but at the same time, I wasn't surprised either. I interpreted the fact that I had not heard from him as a sign that he wasn't interested in knowing more about true love. It wasn't a surprise because once you live like a play-boy, especially for such a long time, it will be hard to change. I had learned that unless people themselves want to change, my words can't change them. When it came to personal behavior of individuals, I had learned to respect views that oppose my own. So I moved on with my life and tried to forget what happened between Justin and I.

CHAPTER SEVEN

One day, Sarah called me on the phone. She said she was going to invite some of her friends over to her townhouse for her birthday, and wanted to see if I was available next Friday night. She had mentioned before that she and her boyfriend had recently started living together, and had rented this nice townhouse in the midtown. I had never been to her place since we met and it sounded like fun. I wasn't going to do anything special that night, so I gladly accepted the invitation.

The day before her birthday party, I called her to see if she wanted me to bring any particular type of food to the party. She insisted that she wanted no one to bring any food at all. She said her closest friend was a strict vegan who could get really offended if there was any type of meat served, and to avoid this, she had decided to cook for everybody. I knew that was going to be a lot of work, so I offered to come and help her with the cooking, putting up the ornaments, and cleaning up afterwards. She refused at first, but since I knew she really needed help but was too shy to accept it, I insisted a second time, and then she accepted it.

I remember it as if it was yesterday. It was sixth of March and the weather was not too hot at all. It was pretty convenient to get to midtown from my place using the public transportation, and that's what I did. On my way, though, I got off the train to buy her a birthday present. I knew she liked dolphins a lot, so I bought her a pair of dolphin-shaped pillows as a gift.

I showed up at her place around 2:00 in the afternoon, and not long after, we both went to the kitchen and started cooking. I had always liked cooking, so it was fun helping my good friend with it. She had already done the grocery shopping, and everything was available, so at least that part was done, but we still had a lot of work to do.

As we were working on the different dishes, we were keeping up a conversation too. We talked about our school, our program, traveling, and many other subjects, until I asked her, "So Sarah, how long have we been friends?"

She was mixing flour, almond milk, and other stuff in a bowl to make some bread dough. Normally, I would use egg whites, but she didn't use any, which I think it was because her friend was a vegan. I knew some vegans who would eat egg whites, but I thought perhaps some more strict ones wouldn't. While doing that, she responded, "Hm, I guess two or three years. How come?"

I said, "Because I wondered if I have ever been introduced to your boyfriend? I mean, you talk about him every now and then, but I don't think I ever got the chance to meet him!"

She said, "Good lord! Are you sure? He's seven feet tall; there is no way you could miss him if you two had met!"

I smiled and sarcastically said, "I'm sorry to break the news, but there are many tall guys out there, Sarah!"

She giggled and said, "You are funny, God bless you!"

I paused for a minute and then said, "You must really like him, don't you? Every time you talk about him, a light shines in your eyes. Did you know that?"

Her cheeks got red and she said, "Yes, I like him. I like him very much!"

I said, "So how long have you been together?"

She said, "A little more than two years."

I said, "If you don't mind me asking, I'm curious to know

how you two met?"

She smiled again and said, "God led us to each other. When God wants two soulmates to find each other, he himself makes it happen. Things come together for it to happen in a way that our minds wouldn't believe. When God wants you to find your soulmate, he will let you feel it in your heart in a way that you just know it!"

I said, "So what's the story? "

At this point, she was done mixing the ingredients of the dough. Then, she took a ceramic tray out of the cabinet and put it on the granite countertop. After pouring some flours on the tray, she grabbed the bread dough and placed it on the tray, kneading it with her bare hands.

She then said, "Well, Adrien and I met at a big Christian conference. The moment I saw him, something in my heart was telling me that he was my soulmate. The man God intended me to be with."

I asked her where she kept her pots. I wanted to boil some water for the vegan dumplings and spaghetti. Then I said, "So what made you think that way?"

She said, "I don't know! It was a feeling. It was like I knew him already for a very long time, like he was the one I was meant to be with. Everything about him was exactly the way my heart had told me my man would be, as if God had already put all the signs in my heart."

Sarah was still hand-kneading the dough, but she seemed to be sweating on that job. I didn't want her to be so tired on her own birthday, so I interrupted her and said, "Sarah, can we switch roles? If you don't mind, I can go on with kneading the dough. I like the exercise."

She said, "Sure if you want to."

After washing my hands one more time, I continued kneading the dough and she took care of frying the vegetables and boiling the water.

She continued, "Where was I? Oh, yeah! So I believe God had put all the signs together for me to know Adrien was my man. That day was a special day from its beginning. It was fall, and weather was heavenly. On the way to the conference, everything looked Godly. It was as if nature was talking to me on behalf of the God to give me the signs. That day, sun was brighter, the wind was milder and the air was softer. Green, red, and yellow leaves were spread on the street like a colorful carpet. Everything that day looked like as if I was in a painting. I just knew God had a message for me that day. I knew I was going to be blessed that day. I had no idea how until I met Adrien. Only then I realized all the signs that day were leading me to him."

She realized the water was boiling, so she poured the veggie dumplings in the pot and started stirring them so that they didn't get stuck together.

She then continued, "The moment I saw him at the conference, my stomach sank! At that first moment I knew he was going to be someone very special in my life. I was always attracted to tall guys, and Asian guys, and he was both—as if God had created him as a perfect fit for me! I wanted to get to know him, but I was so shy to talk to him. I mean, I'm usually a very social person, but when it came to him, suddenly I lost my words. My heart was beating so hard, it felt like it was coming out of my chest. The last time I had felt that sort of strong love was a long time ago when I was a teenager."

While she was pouring the fried vegetables into another dish, she continued, "During one of the breaks after a talk, I asked one of my close friends to introduce me to Adrien even though she didn't know him either. My friend and I approached him. He was talking to another group of people. My friend opened up the conversation with him and then introduced me to him. When Adrien and I shook hands, his hands were firm and strong, but at the same time gentle and warm."

She got another pot to boil more water, then she said, "We chatted a little bit. He seemed to be a very good Christian. He told us about his deep belief in God and how he had devoted himself to serving him and the people. He told us about his journeys to Africa to help the poor children and their families and to preach the Gospel to them as well. Traveling to Africa, helping poor kids, and guiding them to God? That was exactly the man I always wanted! His words were like arrows of love, hitting my heart one by one. I couldn't believe the extreme passion and love I was feeling towards a person I had just met. I know it's crazy to feel that way towards a person you just met, but when love is real, you just know it. Anyway, the conference ended and we all headed back home, but before we left, Adrien ran towards my friend's car and asked if he could add me and my friend on Facebook. He said he liked to stay in touch with the people he had met, but I was hoping he would have the same feelings towards me."

The dough was not sticky anymore, and we had to let it sit for a couple of hours before we put it in the oven. "Sarah, I think this dough is ready. I'm going to work on these veggies over here." I said. We had eggplants, garlic, avocados, broccoli, and potatoes. She had also soaked some chickpeas and beans in water overnight. I thought I could easily make a delicious Falafel out of these vegetables, so I continued, "By the way, Sarah, have you thought about serving Falafel?"

She said, "Oh I love Falafel, but I don't know how to make it. Do you?"

I said, "Yeah, for sure! It's pretty simple now that you were smart enough to soak chickpeas the night before."

She giggled, "I was soaking them to be served just like that, maybe as an appetizer, but sure, I like the idea of Falafel better!"

I smiled and said, "Alright then! Falafel, it is!"

I asked for some scallions and parsley. After adding all the ingredients, I asked her, "So Sarah, what happened next with you and Adrien?"

She said, "After he added us on Facebook, I didn't hear from him for a while. But one day, he sent a message. We went on a date soon after. He was unbelievably good at every little thing a girl loves to see on a date. First of all, he didn't take me to one of those boring dinner dates. On the first date, we grabbed food at an international food truck festival. I tried so many different types of foods that I loved. Then, we went to see the football game between the Houston Texans, my favorite team of all, and the New York Giants. He ended the night by taking me to a nice wine bar, where we drank a little and talked. He was making me laugh so hard, but at the same time, he never went too far with any of his jokes. He was so good at keeping eye contact and keeping me emotionally engaged, not to mention the way he kept the conversation going. I mean our conversations felt so natural and smooth that I didn't feel the time passing at all. Everything was so good, as if he knew me for thousands of years. After a month, we announced our relationship to our close friends and since then, we've been in the loveliest relationship ever. He treats me like a princess. He really is God's gift to me."

I didn't let her know what I really thought about her feelings towards Adrien. My understanding of what she said was that she had based her relationship on sparks, but who was I to judge? I decided not to say a word. Whether based on sparks or not, their relationship seemed to be working, so I thought I shouldn't discourage her in any way.

Only, I asked in a joking way, "So it's all flowers and rainbows?"

She smiled and said, "No, there are problems. He sometimes doesn't listen to me or doesn't follow through on his promises. Also, sometimes he agrees with me in words even though I know he doesn't mean it, but all I need is to look into his gorgeous eyes; I feel so much love that I forget all the problems and give him another chance."

I changed the subject and we continued to chat and cook like that for another hour or so. Soon, we had many different dishes and desserts ready for the guests. The guests showed up one after another, and gradually the living room was filled with people. Sarah's favorite music was on. The finger foods we made turned out great. The entire living room was filled with laughter, joy, and happiness.

In the middle of the party, Sarah came to me, and asked if I wanted to be introduced to her best friend, Rebecca. Sarah said her friend had tried the Falafel I made and was amazed by the texture and the taste. She said her friend was asking if I could share the recipe with her. So I followed Sarah to be introduced to her vegan best friend, Rebecca.

When we got near Rebecca, she was talking to another guest. Once they finished talking, Sarah looked at Rebecca and said, "Rebecca, I'd like to introduce my friend, Hadi!"

Then Rebecca looked at me and while shaking hands she said, "So you are the Falafel master, right?"

I laughed and said, "Well, I don't know if I'd put it that way, but yes, I helped Sarah make them."

Sarah said, "Oh don't be too humble! You made them from scratch! I had no idea how to make Falafels at all!"

So I looked at Rebecca and I said, "Sarah told me you were interested in knowing the recipe. I'd be happy to share."

Rebecca said, "Yeah, I make it all the time, but I have never had one so crunchy and delicious. These are yummy!"

Sarah politely excused herself from the conversation to make sure all the guests were enjoying themselves. Then I explained the recipe and my own cooking tricks to Rebecca. Afterwards, just to have a bit of social conversation with her, I asked, "So Rebecca, how do you know Sarah?"

She answered, "We were high school best friends. How do you know her?"

I said, "Sarah and I are both chemical engineering PhD students at the same school. We used to be classmates for a few courses but now we are doing our own research in different research groups."

She said, "And where are you from?"

I answered, "Saudi Arabia!"

She said, "Oh okay. Well, nice meeting you!" and then she left to get a drink.

The music was remarkable. Everyone was happy. I was having a good time too. Soon, they brought the birthday cake. Sarah blew out the candles on the cake and then kissed the tall Asian guy who was sitting beside her. I could guess that he was Adrien. The more I looked at him, the more I thought I recognized him as the same person I saw at Justin's house party—the guy who was hugging and kissing the naked girl. However, I couldn't be sure. I thought I must be wrong.

Sarah opened the gifts one by one. She seemed to be extremely happy to have all these people around her, especially her boyfriend. After that, Sarah started to cut the cake and share pieces among the guests. I liked the cake a lot.

A few hours passed and all the guests had left. I stayed to help her wash the dishes and clean up. After that, Sarah said, "Hey Hadi, let me introduce you to Adrien. I don't want you to leave this house without officially being introduced to him!"

I said, "Sure Sarah, I would love to meet him." I could have spilled it out that I might have met him another night at a crazy party, but I resisted that urge. Why? Maybe I was wrong. Maybe it wasn't him. I didn't want to destroy their good relationship based on a speculation like that. Sarah led the way and I followed her. She was going around the living room and the patio to see if Adrien was there, but she wasn't able to find him. She said, "I don't know where he is now." She then took me upstairs. I wasn't comfortable going upstairs to their bedrooms, so I said, "Sarah, it's okay. Maybe he is sleeping or something and I don't want to interrupt him just to get introduced."

Sarah said, "No, it's ok. I insist you two should be introduced tonight."

She opened the door to the bedroom, only to see her imaginary love bubble burst.

Adrien was having sex on Sarah's bed with another girl, who seemed to be one of the guests they both knew. I didn't know her, but I had seen Sarah talking to her earlier during the party, so she knew her. I was surprised but poor Sarah, she was beyond shocked! She was just standing right there at the door with her eyes closed and her hands on her mouth. I could see the silent tears finding their way down her cheeks from her eyes.

Adrien, who knew there was no way to explain this, grabbed his clothes at the drop of a hat and quickly left the house, and so did the girl.

I helped Sarah sit on the couch. She was not talking to me. She was just staring straight ahead. She was shocked. I stayed for an hour to see if she would get better. It was getting late. Although I didn't want to leave Sarah like that, it wasn't proper for me to stay so late in the night.

I searched for Sarah's phone and found Rebecca's phone number. She had left earlier before we found Adrien. I called her number. She was asleep. I explained to her what had happened and that I thought it would be good for Sarah if she could stay with her for the night. She was angry at Adrien and started cussing at him over the phone. She then said she would show up soon at Sarah's place. When she arrived and I made sure Sarah was in good hands, I left.

I really felt bad for Sarah. She didn't deserve any of this. Her kind and genuine heart was completely broken and she was shocked. Of course, she was the victim in her relationship with this guy and there was no blame on her for what Adrien had done to her. But at the same time, a question had filled my mind that night: *When she chose Adrien based on sparks, why didn't she see it could end badly?*

I mean, when you follow the spark mindset, the guy who you end up with may or may not be the one who actually could offer you true happiness. She had chosen Adrien based on his height, the way his face looked, the way he talked, the adventures he had in life, and many other unimportant things that could have led to that spark in her heart. Little did she know that when you select your love based on sparks, you might be missing some of the things that truly matter.

Perhaps she thought when she found someone she felt so passionate about, she then could make him loyal, kind, and honest, or in other words, she thought she could later change the person she had sparks with. This is such a mistake, though. You can't change anyone, unless they first internalize the change themselves! I was thinking in my head out of compassion for her, *why didn't she base her love on the qualities that truly matter, and then let the spark happen over time? Wouldn't it have been better to find an honest, kind, loyal, and understanding true lover and then let the time create sparks gradually?*

Anyway, it had been a very long day! I went to bed right after getting home. The day after, I texted Rebecca to check on Sarah's situation. I didn't want to call Sarah yet because she probably needed some space after that terrible shock.

A few days passed and Rebecca had not yet responded. Sarah had not shown up in her research group, either. I knew because I bumped into her PhD adviser in the Chemical Engineering Department. I asked him about Sarah to see if he knew how she was doing. All he told me was that she had called him, asking for some personal time off. I was getting really concerned for her, and so I decided to pay a visit to her apartment.

After I was done that day in our research lab, I went home, took a shower, changed clothes, and headed towards her apartment again. It was an hour before sunset when I got there. I was going for the doorbell, but before I could ring it, I noticed a letter was placed on the door mat. I picked it up. On the back of the letter, it was written with ink, "I am sorry for my mistake." And it was signed, "Sincerely, Adrien."

Immediately I realized that this must be an apology letter from Adrien. How dare this guy thought he could simply cheat on this poor girl right in front of her eyes on her birthday, and would ever be able to compensate for it with an apology letter?!

At first, I wanted to just rip that letter apart and would never tell Sarah about it, but then I thought, *it is her decision, not mine, to do whatever she wants with that letter.* So I rang the doorbell. I did it a few times, and no one showed up at the door. I began to walk away, thinking that perhaps she was out, but suddenly I heard someone open the door. It was Rebecca, and she said, "Oh, it's you!"

I walked back towards the door, but she was blocking the entrance to the apartment by holding the door frame and standing right in the way. I stayed closer to the door and said, "I rang the doorbell a few times and thought she might not be home. I hope I didn't wake you guys up. By the way, I didn't know you were here too. It's so kind of you to stay here with Sarah so that she doesn't have to be alone in these tough times she is having."

She said, "She is taking a nap now, and yeah, I decided to stay here with her for a while. This poor girl was shocked as hell that night. You know? As a boy, maybe it's difficult for you to understand, but it's devastating to see that someone you loved so dearly would cheat on you in your own bed, so I don't think it's a good idea for you to see her right now. Sorry, but I think you'd better leave."

I said, "I think I understand that perfectly Rebecca, and you may be right that I would be better off going. I was just really concerned about how she was doing, and since I could not get ahold of her in any other way, I thought I would stop by and visit her. Anyway, thanks for updating me and please take a good care of her. Oh and by the way, this is a letter I found on the doormat."

I handed over the letter to Rebecca, and turned to leave again. But I hadn't taken the second step before I heard Sarah yelling from her room on second floor, "Who is it, Rebecca? Is someone at the door?"

Rebecca said, "No one, bestie! Just go back to bed!"

Sarah said, "No, I know there is someone at the door! Who is it?"

Rebecca looked at me in a blameful way as if it was my fault that Sarah was now awake. She was running downstairs with quick, heavy steps that we could easily hear from the door. Perhaps she thought it was Adrien at the door, and that was her hurry. When she saw it was me at the door, she suddenly lost momentum, and said only one sentence, "Oh, it's you Hadi!"

As she was now slowly walking down the stairs, I responded, "Hi Sarah, I was a bit concerned for you. I texted you and Rebecca, but I got no response. I also realized you were skipping school, so as a friend, I thought I should check on you. How are you?"

Rebecca looked at me once again with an obviously

annoyed face that said this question was inappropriate or maybe stupid. In retrospect, she was right and that was a stupid question, but I was there to know how she was feeling. I was genuinely worried for her. She was a good friend of mine and this was a very hard time for her, so I wanted to be there for her with any help I could possibly give.

Sarah said, "I am…" she paused and I could see tears in her eyes banking, "spectacular!"

Then suddenly she realized Rebecca was holding the letter I gave her. She said with extreme curiosity, "What is that?"

Rebecca said, "Oh, this? It's nothing! Nothing important at all!"

Sarah wildly grabbed the letter from Rebecca's hand and ran upstairs while opening the letter. Rebecca chased her, trying to keep her from opening it. I closed the door and followed them upstairs. When I got upstairs, I saw that letter wrinkled on the floor. Sarah had broken down on the ground with her both hands on her face, crying out like a cloud in spring time. Rebecca was holding her shoulders, trying to calm her.

When Rebecca saw me upstairs, she looked at me and said in a very angry voice, "Is this what you wanted? I told you to leave, didn't I?"

I had no response to give to that, so I remained silent. In fact, the entire room remained in a deadly silence. The only sound was Sarah's sobbing.

After about half an hour, she dried the tears off her face, picked the wrinkled letter off the ground, and said to Rebecca, "I want you to read this out loud."

Rebecca said, "Sarah, No! That's really not a good idea! Look at yourself—you deserve happiness and joy, not so much pain! You don't need to know what nonsense he has written for you, you need to give up any love and love only yourself; that's what you need, not this letter."

Sarah almost yelled, "I'm telling you to read it! Sorry, but please read it!" She then sat on the arm chair. Rebecca and I took a seat too.

Rebecca said, "Okay, if that's what you really want. Don' say I didn't warn you! I'm sure he is only looking to trick you and break your heart one more time; guys are all the same shit!"

She opened the letter and started reading it:

Dearest Sarah,

What I did to you is unforgivable, and I don't mean to make any excuses anymore, but I think at least you deserve to know how things ended up that way.

As you know, I was brought up on a farm in south Texas, a typical farming family, but there is a little detail I never told you about my childhood. My dad had the habit of getting hammered almost every night, and then beating us to death, especially my mom. I was raised in a house filled with violence, abuse, and fear. When I was fifteen years old, I packed everything I could in a backpack, stole some cash from my mom, and left home to never come back. Of course, soon I ran out of money and became homeless. A lot happened to me during that time, but long story short, one day I met a priest who changed the course of my life. He gave me food, a place to live, and a little cash in return for working in his church as a missionary. I didn't really believe in any religion, but in order to survive, I had to pretend. Soon I found that, by lying, I could make people like me. I could escape my fears.

The truth is when I met you, I wasn't totally honest either. I am very ashamed of admitting it, but remember how on the first few dates you and I found so much in common? Well, most of what I said was a lie. I just said what I thought would make you like me.

But things are different now. I have changed. Before I met you, my life was full of fear and lies. I didn't mean to use you; I was just scared of being alone. But I was scared of being with one person too, because what if it didn't work out? What if that person stopped loving me? If I only loved one person, I could lose everything.

But after some time in a relationship with you, you showed me how to love, even though I wasn't a good boyfriend, or even a good person, really. I promise you, Sarah, if you give me another chance, I want to be honest and loving this time. This time I'll be brave. I promise you this time will be different. I thought if I honestly admitted all the lies I have told you in the past, maybe you'd believe me that I want to change. I know this is a lot to handle, but please give me another chance to start over.

Sincerely and apologetically,
Adrien

CHAPTER EIGHT

During the entire time Rebecca was reading Adrien's letter, Sarah was worryingly quiet. She had curled up on the cozy armchair in the corner of the room. Her eyes were fixed on the ceiling in a way that looked like she was reviewing the past in her head. I could see tears banking up in her eyes every once in a while, but she would quietly dry her eyes with a napkin. I was worried for her. I was also extremely sad that loving the wrong person turned my happy friend into this sad crying soul.

Rebecca, on the other hand, looked livid. She looked at Sarah and then me and said with an attitude, "Thanks a lot Hadi! Is this what you wanted? Here is a tip: next time don't touch what isn't yours!"

I said, "I don't think this is entirely my fault, but I apologize if I unintentionally made you sad, Sarah."

"Yeah, you better be sorry. Guys are all the same!" Rebecca mumbled under her breath. She went to the kitchen and came back with a pack of beer. She put the pack on the table, looked at Sarah and said, "Hey bestie! Do you want to grab a beer with me? It'll relax you a bit."

Without saying a word or even looking at her, Sarah refused by nodding her head. Then Rebecca opened up a bottle for herself, sat on the same spot she was sitting before, and started to chug on the beer.

I said, "With all due respect, Rebecca, I think you are wrong when you say all guys are the same. There are really good guys out there too."

She sneeringly laughed and said in a sarcastic tone, "Yeah, if you say so!"

Silence persisted for a while, as I guess none of us had anything to say, until Sarah abruptly said, "Maybe I should give him another chance."

Rebecca looked at her with a face I will never forget: her jaw dropped, her eyes wide open, and her eyebrows raised. She said, "Oh God, kill me now! I can't believe you! That son-of-a-bitch got caught cheating right in your own bed and now you are contemplating giving him another chance? Seriously?"

Sarah responded in an anxious voice, "I know. I know he cheated. But even though part of me hates him for that, another part of me wants to sympathize with him. Maybe he really wants to change now."

Rebecca's face had turned red. She said with in an indignant tone, "Are you kidding me? Sarah, guys are all the same! They lie and cheat and once they finally lose you, they promise changes that never happen. Don't you tell me you believe his lies, okay?"

Sarah answered, "Well obviously, I have been believing his lies for a few years now."

I said, "I don't agree with Rebecca when she says all guys are the same, but Sarah, I think she has a point here. Do you think if you give him another chance, he is going to magically change? I know that happens in movies a lot, but you know, people don't easily change in real life. In my culture, we say testing what has already been tested means you don't trust your eyes."

Sarah said, "Look, I'm not stupid. I know he is probably saying all this just to get me back, but what if he's not? What if he really is going to change? I kind of sympathize with him. He has had a life full of fear and now maybe he has realized that no love can happen with fear and wants to change."

I said, "Sarah, we all have fears. You know? For the longest time, I have felt fear in the core of my bone. The idea of living in a country where I don't know anyone, or the thought that I might grow old alone if I continue not to settle for anything but true love all are very scary, but not every guy chooses to lie and cheat in the face of those fears. It's one thing to have fears, but it's another if you base your relationships on it. There are good men out there who'd rather be alone than play with someone's emotions."

Sarah said, "But Hadi, I did start my relationship with Adrien based on the same love you are talking about, and this is my life now! Look at me! I'm a mess!" she continued sobbing.

I thought in my head that in reality, Sarah was blinded by her initial attraction to Adrien—by the sparks. But considering the situation, I didn't put that thought into words. I just simply said, "Well, Sarah, true love has to be two-sided, you know?"

"Maybe you are right. And now that I've read this letter, I feel like I never even knew him at all. So maybe it wasn't love. I don't know." Sarah said while continuing to shed tears.

Rebecca looked at Sarah with a disappointed face and said, "Bestie!! Come on! Let me open a beer for you. No guy is worth making yourself sad for. There are plenty of fish in the sea." Then she looked at me and said, "Could you please stop making it worse? Oh my God! Can't you see her situation?!"

I raised both my hands up as if in surrender, and said, "Rebecca, I'm not trying to make her sad or anything. In my opinion, Adrien's lies are rooted in fear. When it comes to love, many people act out of fear, whether it be fear of social isolation, fear of being alone, fear of how their friends judge them, and so on. But I believe the true lovers don't let fears rule them. That's all I said."

Rebecca said in an annoyed tone, "You guys all talk about true love in the beginning and then you turn around and do the same shit. This is not the time! Sarah doesn't need to hear your opinions on love right now. Actually, neither of us do. So do us a favor and keep them to yourself, okay?"

Sarah looked at Rebecca and said, "Rebecca! I think you are being a little mean to him. Let the guy talk!"

Rebecca said, "But, it's not the right…"

Sarah interrupted her and said, "Look, maybe you don't want to hear him, but I do. I have been thinking nonstop over these last few days, and still can't figure out why on earth this happened to me. Maybe he can give me a clue, so let him talk."

Rebecca shook her head in exasperation, but didn't say anything.

Sarah got off that armchair she was sitting on and sat on the couch right in front of me and then said, "So, how should I know if I have found this two-sided true love you are talking about? Because that's what I thought I had with Adrien."

I said, "I think true love is a fruit of a certain selfless mindset. You know? I have come to the conclusion that the root cause of problems in today's romantic relationships is more in our mindsets than methods. Our mindsets play a role throughout the dating process, even right at the beginning when you select a partner, but also later on and even after marriage. Being in a relationship with mutual egoless mindset is the key in determining how successful a relationship is."

Sarah interrupted me in an impatient voice and said, "Hadi! Make it short and in layman's terms! Please! I'm not in the most patient mood!"

I continued, "Okay, Sarah. True love is a lifestyle based on a selfless mindset. It is not a feeling, like the initial sparks of attraction are; true love is a decision, a choice. It's a choice to always consider your love to be the other half of yourself and it needs to be mutual. If you want to find someone who can love you selflessly, you should understand that such person may not necessarily make you feel those sparks—the immediate attraction you fantasize about—at least in the beginning."

"True love doesn't have to start with a spark. Now sometimes strong sparks make you feel you have true love, but because sparks are feelings and subject to our mood, the sacrifices and selflessness rooting from sparks does not last forever. All feelings are doomed to end! There is so much to say about true love, Sarah, so this is as concise as I can possibly put it."

Sarah said, "Maybe I did choose Adrien based on those sparks you are talking about, but it wasn't like I gave my heart to him overnight. We were dating for about two years now. Everything with him was so sweet! I thought I knew him so well. I thought I knew his heart. I was so proud of myself for capturing him for myself, but all of a sudden, that bouncy castle I had made in my mind out of him blew up with the tip of a needle!" She had a lump in her throat while saying this, but resisted letting it out by crying.

It was truly hurtful for me to see my good friend heartbroken like that, but there wasn't anything anyone could do anymore. I asked, "Sarah, are you sure you really want to talk about this right now? On a second thought, maybe Rebecca is right that this is not the best time to talk to you about this."

She said, "God bless your heart! Yes, I'm sure. It makes me feel better to know why things went wrong."

She continued, "But Hadi, this sounds a bit counterintuitive to me. How can I fall in love without any sparks?"

I said, "Let me emphasize that I am not saying sparks are bad. All I'm trying to say is that it should not be the foundation of a relationship. When you are selecting someone to date, if you base your selection on sparks right off the bat and only consider guys who give you sparks on the first few dates, then you might miss out on a guy who can truly and deeply appreciate you. A true lover is committed to always loving you with loyalty, understanding, and kindness forever. The key to the solution is time. Rather than spending your time exclusively with someone who you have a crush on, take it slow. Give everyone a chance, get to know them in depth to understand their mindsets, to know their intentions, regardless of whether you feel sparks with them or not. Time sometimes helps create sparks that were not necessarily there in the beginning. In contrast, simply giving more time isn't going to make a dishonest person suddenly honest or a selfish person a true lover."

Sarah didn't say anything, just curled up on the couch in a way that seemed like she was reviewing the sequence of events that happened between Adrien and her.

Rebecca, however, could not remain silent anymore. She started talking in a calm voice but as she continued to talk, her voice was becoming louder and her face was getting more intense.

"Do you really think that kind of love actually exists? If you do, let me break the news to you: I think you are extremely naive. Humans are selfish at their core. Actually, selfishness is humanity's oldest evolutionary trait; it doesn't go away so easily! Let me ask you: how many other people have you found who believe in the same selfless love you preach? Do you even believe in it yourself? Because it sounds like the kind of romantic bullshit guys say just to get into girls' pants. How do we know if you aren't faking it?"

At this point, I got really irritated and lost my patience a bit, so I said firmly, "I don't care even a bit what people like you think of me! I have always deeply believed in the type of egoless true love I preach! You want to call me naïve, stupid, or anything else, go ahead! But don't accuse me of not believing in what I say!"

I paused for a few seconds and calmed myself. Then I continued, "But you are right that not so many people want to base their actions on this type of egoless love anymore. That's the most unfortunate. I know for a fact that true love exists because it at least exists in my own heart. I can't prove that fact to anyone in a short time, but I'm sure in the long run, they can see the deep and purified true love in my heart. I'm also sure the core of true love exists somewhere in the heart of all humans. Why does it not show itself in their behavior? Maybe because they learn to suppress it; I don't know. But it does exist! Believe me!"

She said, "Okay, maybe you genuinely believe in what you say, and I can respect that, but here is my question: why should we even bother? Look, love may be a nice thing sometimes but look how painful it can be! We don't need love to have a great life! Everyone is trying so hard to get this thing they call love, while there is a whole life ahead of us to enjoy. Women can be very happy on their own. The whole love story with Mr. Right has an expiration date—maybe one night, one week, one year, or one decade, but at the end of the day, women are nothing but toys to most guys. At the end, all we have is the pain you guys leave us with; the pain of being used and played with like toys. We don't need this bullshit. We deserve a great life."

I answered, "There are two types of pain in romantic relationships. One kind is a pain that is outside anyone's control and sometimes inevitable. Another pain is the result of our own mistakes, which can be avoided. This latter kind of pain shows up sooner or later in a relationship because you choose the wrong person even though at the time you might have thought this person was right for you, but please don't blame this on love. If you put your faith in the wrong person because of the sparks they give you or the fears you might have, then it is not fair to blame it on love. When you really like someone, you trust them with the deepest part of your heart and of course, this makes you vulnerable. Now if that person is all about his own ego, at some point, he will break your heart because he prefers his own self-interest over yours. But if you select a partner based on the principles of egoless love and not those of spark, fear, or exchange mindsets, there is a good chance you'll find true love. I mean, in life you only get what you look for. If you look for sparks, you get them. There are good guys out there who would never leave you, who are with you in the good and bad of life. That's true love. It may not start with sparks, though. They may not be necessarily the guys who make you go wow, but if you give them a chance, just a chance to get to know them, you find true love.

But when you say women don't need anyone to make them happy, or when you say women deserve a great life, I couldn't agree with you more. I think we all deserve a great life; we all deserve to feel happy. Every being deserves love. And the plain truth is that no one can make you happy if you are not happy on your own."

Rebecca raised her hands above her head, looked at Sarah, and said, "Amen to that! But you see? You just admitted it—no one but yourself can make you happy. So even if you ever find the right person, it doesn't make you happy. So if you love yourself, why would you need anyone else?!"

I said, "Hold on a second! I think you misunderstood what I meant. True love can't create absolute happiness, but it can make you a lot happier. Look, I never said having a boyfriend or a girlfriend, a husband or a wife, or having children can make you happy. What I am saying is that having a relationship based on egoless love mindset can enlighten you through all the kindness, contentment, peace and above all sacrifices that you go through to make that true love last. True love uplifts the soul and makes the true lovers better, healthier, and happier people."

For the first time, Rebecca did not come back to me with another answer. It was as if the idea of true love finally clicked in her mind and she started to truly think about it. I asked Rebecca a more sensitive question, "By the way, what do you think makes you not look for love? Do you think it might be fear? Fear of perhaps a relationship failure and the broken heart that follows afterwards?"

She scoffed, but her voice sounded softer when she said, "I don't know you well enough to talk about that! That's my personal life."

I continued, "Okay, fair enough. There are many kinds of fears that we all have to wrestle with before we can reach anything valuable. I never said it's easy but it's necessary. Adrien's fear of living alone made him selfishly fake love and he ended up hurting Sarah. Fear has perhaps as many variations as the number of living humans. Our fears either create a comfort zone, making us scared of change, or they make us do foolish and selfish things. But we all need to manage our fears if we want to move towards true love. Everyone has a different story of how their heart was broken, and let me tell you, I am no exception. My heart has been broken many times, but at the end, I choose to control my fears and try love again and again, but each time I learn from the mistakes of the past. That's how we grow as humans, isn't it?"

A kind of deep silence ruled our conversation for a few minutes. This was definitely a good sign. A sign that they started to digest and internalize what was told about the true love.

It was already a long and intense conversation and considering the terrible thing that had happened to Sarah, I realized I'd better stop talking about love and let her rest. It takes time for a broken heart to heal, but in my heart I really hoped that what I told her would make her next relationship more successful.

I said, "Alright, it's getting late and I have to study for an exam next Monday. I really hope you recover very soon, Sarah. I know you let me know if I can be of any help."

Sarah kindly walked me to the door and said goodbye. I walked back home, really wishing for everyone from the depth of my heart that one day we all find real love.

CHAPTER NINE

R oughly six months had passed since Sarah's birthday night. Time is the greatest remedy for many pains and so it was for Sarah's broken heart. I was so happy to see she was gradually recovering.

One day when I was passing through the corridors of her research lab to get to my professor's office, we ran into each other. After our usual chit-chat, she said, "By the way Hadi, what do you think about giving a talk on the subject of love at a conference?"

"A conference? What kind of conference do you mean?" I asked curiously.

She replied, "It's a conference about marriage and relationships. Like I've told you before, after what happened between me and Adrien, I've been trying to learn more about love, so I've been keeping an eye out for any places hosting events where they discuss topics like psychology and love. One of these places is a cool cultural space, called IPH. One of their volunteering board members is my friend. She told me they are planning to set up a conference on relationships and are looking for speakers. Guess who I immediately thought of? I thought, if you are interested, this could be a good time for you to talk about your ideas to a broader public."

That was a little out of blue, but I said, "Thank you Sarah.

This sounds like a great opportunity, but how about I think about it and let you know?"

She said, "Yeah, for sure. Text me the title of your talk if you are up for it. I'll also make sure to send you the other details. Got to go to run an experiment now, but see you around." And so we both departed on our ways.

After some thinking, I decided to go through with the conference. Later on, she sent me the electronic brochure of the program along with the speaker invitation letter, and other information about the conference in an email. I looked up their social media page. A little over a thousand people had signed up, so it was way more popular than I had ever expected. IPH, the name of the sponsoring organization, stood for the Interfaith Partnership of Houston, which was a non-profit organization with the goal of religious tolerance. The event was supposed to be held in an auditorium in their main building in downtown within a month. They had done a great job advertising it to different groups around the city with diverse backgrounds. They had advertised to mosques, churches, synagogues, universities, and so on to make sure a diverse group of people would show up for the event.

I was happy, but at the same time a bit stressed. I was happy because this could give me an amazing opportunity to be able to spread the word of love to a diverse audience. At the same time, it was a bit scary because I had never given a public speech in front of such a big crowd.

Anyway, I sent her the title of my talk: "The Three Forbidden T's of Love"

She texted back, "That's a pretty catchy title! Looking forward to it."

Time flew by until the day of the workshop. Per my usual habit, I got there a little earlier than necessary, but the crowd was already huge. Seeing that huge crowd exacerbated both my excitement and fear of public speaking at the same time, which was an electrifying mix of feelings. I knew my talk was scheduled for 3 pm for half an hour. I got one of the flyers from the reception table and it showed the title of my talk,

"The Three Forbidden T's of Love" right next to my name, "Dr. Hadi Shamsi". That brought a smile to my face. *I'm not a doctor yet, at least not till I defend my PhD thesis*, but then I thought, *probably no one cares, so why not?!* reminding myself to be more confident, something I was trying to improve on.

After waiting a little bit, it was my time to speak. The announcer introduced me and I walked out onto the stage among all the applauding.

The auditorium was pretty big, but from the stage, it looked like a freaking stadium, thanks to my fear of public speaking. The hall was completely packed. I didn't have the exact count, but it seemed to be way more than a thousand people. Many were seated on the neatly organized rows of white plastic chairs, and some were standing on their feet in the back.

When I walked on the stage, I looked down the floor for a few seconds, trying to find a better line to start my talk with; then, I looked at the crowd and said, "How are we doing today?"

The crowd mumbled, "Good."

I said, "You may have noticed that for a few seconds I was just walking on the stage without talking, pondering about something. There is a fundamental question that I want to ask the audience here to try to answer: We are here to talk about love and marriage, but in all honesty, what is this love that everyone talks about?"

For a couple of long awkward moments, I was looking at the crowd and they were staring back at me. They seemed confused about what I was asking them, so I broke the silence and rephrased my question, "I want you to reflect inside for a second and ask yourself what is your end goal in a relationship? What do you call love? Anyone who wants to answer can raise their hand."

A girl in the back raised her hand. I pointed at her and she answered, "Love is a feeling of attraction towards someone, like when you have a crush on someone."

I said, "Thank you. Anyone else?" After that girl showed

courage by raising her hand, a few other people raised theirs.

A guy in the front row said, "It doesn't necessarily have to be towards a person. You can love your pet, your job, your car, or anything of that sort!"

Now more and more people in the audience were finding the courage to raise their hands and express their opinions. An old lady who was seated in one of the middle row seats stood up and spoke without raising her hand, "My late husband was the love of my life. God bless him! He passed away four years ago and I miss him a lot. I have my children and grandchildren around but I have to live with his memories. That's what love is! To miss your love even after half century of living together!" and then she slowly sat back in her seat.

At this point, the hands of almost everyone in the room were up. Now they all wanted to say what they thought love was.

I said, "Thanks everyone! I can see many hands are up and that's great. What it means is that you all have your own definition of what love is and I think it might be a bit different from each person to the next. Defining love for a lot of us is one of those things that can never be done perfectly because it's just not easy to put it into words. Every time you try to define it in words, it feels like you could have done a better job."

On the podium on the other side of the stage, there was a glass of water. I walked towards it and took a sip and then continued, "We all have our differences, but I do strongly believe that, deep within, we all are looking for one thing when it comes to love. We intrinsically know and crave that type of love deep within—the kind of love that is selfless, consistent, and deep. But let's think about it: why is it that we sometimes have so many problems finding that true love in practice? Why is it that many relationships or even marriages fail? I mean, you would think when two people get married, they do it because they want to spend the rest of their lives together, right? So what really happens to that initial fiery love after some time? Was it ever love to begin with? Maybe we mix up that pure and sacred source of true love with other mindsets. Maybe we confuse ourselves on what love is and where to find it. I don't have enough time today to go into this deeply, but I wanted to start my talk with an open question for the audience. There is something very important to think about when you go home."

"So the main thing that I want to talk about today is what I call *The Three Forbidden T's of Love*. The three deadly sins of true love are Trying love casually, Timing love, and Taking love for granted."

I continued, "These three forbidden T's are common mistakes that I see tons of people make when looking for love. Many people focus on learning behavioral techniques to avoid these bad habits without actually correcting their mindsets, which turns out to be really difficult. Bad mindsets are to bad habits as the virus is to the symptoms. Learning techniques is good, but once the mindset is purified to love, I'd like to think that good habits follow naturally. Committing these T's shows a lack of enough belief in true love. In my mind, there is nothing in the world more sacred than true love, and therefore, true love deserves respect. I'm not saying true lovers never make mistakes; they do, but they really try to learn from their mistakes. Anyway, let's dig into the details of each of the three T's one by one:"

"The first forbidden T is Trying love casually. It can have many different manifestations, but one example is casually jumping from one relationship to another without seriously loving that person. When you treat relationships casually, you like the idea of being with a person. Even further, you may like that person while he or she is young, beautiful, happy, and accommodating your needs in a relationship. But in the end, you are not ready to love; you are not ready to sacrifice and compromise. I have seen so many girls and boys who are in relationships with someone they don't truly love, and then if it doesn't work out, they have no worries at all—they move on to the next one right away. They might have fun and good times and like each other, but they are not serious about truly loving each other.

Now, I genuinely believe in free will. It is their choice to be casual as an individual. But my sincere fear for our society is that increasingly more people treat relationships casually. I hope I am exaggerating, but perhaps the time is not far ahead of us when all that will remain is short-term casual relationships or even longer relationships where people have one foot out the door, always keeping their eyes open for something better to come along. I am afraid that in such a society, it would be abnormal to be a true lover, so finding someone who really believes in true love would be like finding a needle in a haystack.

Along this line, there is this common casual mindset out there that if I'm young, I don't need to care about true love. I can have fun for now and when I get older, then I'll try to find something meaningful. In my humble opinion, and based on all the interviews I have done, there is a problem with such thought process: you might be missing out on a true lover who is really ready to love you wholeheartedly while you are in a casual relationship. A true lover will never approach you to ask you out on a date if he or she knows you are in a relationship because they respect that you are with someone, even if they really like you. Since you continue to casually jump from one partner to another, the true lover most likely will never find a good chance to tell you how they feel and they will eventually move on. So, you will lose one opportunity to find someone with true and genuine love, and who knows if there will be another chance in life or not?"

A tall middle-aged guy from the audience stood up from his chair and said, "I'm sorry I'm interrupting your talk. It's just that every word of what you said sounded like music to my ears. I have a son who thinks that way and won't listen to my advice. My question for you is what you suggest I do to convince him that kind of lifestyle doesn't end well?"

I asked, "What is your name, sir?"

He said, "Michael."

I said, "Michael, I think that is a great question. I would be happy to discuss that with you after the talk, but in short, I don't think we can force beliefs on anyone. Some people may not really want to change, and that's okay, even if we don't agree with them. I think words of advice like this can only help people who want to change but don't know how. Does that make sense?"

He said, "Absolutely! Thanks," and sat down back on his chair.

I continued, "The second forbidden T is Timing love. Again, this can have many manifestations, but generally this means expecting love to happen only in certain periods of your life when you are ready for it. In other words, rejecting any possibility of love when you don't expect it or you don't feel ready for it. I hate to break the news to those people, but life, in general, doesn't work that way. Life doesn't wait for us to get completely ready for receiving what it has to offer. If life offers the beauty of true love to us and we reject it because we have some other priority, it is possible that it might never happen again."

"This T, like the first T, is sometimes rooted in not realizing the sacredness and beauty of true love and therefore, not respecting it as we should. Sometimes, people put so many things first in their lives and the last is love. They are always busy reaching this or that goal, while happiness truly comes from enriched, healthy, and flourishing soul rather than what belongings or titles you might possess, and I have found nothing more effective than true love to enrich our souls."

"Another point is that a healthy and genuine kind of true love often does not interfere with other goals that we want to accomplish; in fact, it can be of great help towards them. But my message is try not to time love. Try to understand how true love can bring true happiness and so be open to it at any point in your life, no matter what other things are going on."

"Except, of course, if you are married or already in love with someone in which case, I wouldn't advise fooling around."

The audience laughed out loud.

I continued, "The third and final forbidden T is Taking

love for granted. Just like the other two T's, this may also come from not deeply appreciating or knowing the importance of true love. It is perhaps the nature of human beings to get used to anything in their lives when they don't constantly remind themselves of its importance. The point is we can get used to our loved ones and take them for granted."

"Those who recognize the value of true love choose to never take that true love for granted. They love their loved ones every single day as if it is the last day they are blessed with each other. They work for the happiness of their loved ones as if this is the last thing they have the chance to do for them. The essence of love never runs out or gets rusty for those who choose to appreciate this love continuously and selflessly."

"Time is the key. I'll tell you what I have done and still do when searching for my own love. I would neither abruptly act on crushes, nor reject anyone who doesn't immediately attract me. I get to know everyone around me as friends until I find someone who believes in true love in their actions. I don't jump into a relationship quickly out of the fear of being alone or the fear of how others might think of me. In fact, I have no fear of staying single until I see the possibility of a true love. A type of love that is not based on infatuation or give and take, but based on a constant journey of selflessness, which I have called the Egoless mindset. I consider everyone but at the same time, I ask this fundamental question: why is that person interested in me and why am I interested in her? I don't want to be with someone who likes me only because of my looks, because obviously that goes away. I don't want to be with someone who likes me for an image they have created of me that is not really me. I want someone whose love is true. This sincerely genuine, internal, and eternal ability to fight for someone is a choice that I call true love. When I think I have found someone who also believes in true love, I would definitely start dating her to see if what we have really is genuine true love. I'm not afraid of failure or my heart being broken. If in the process my heart gets broken, well, it's unfortunate, but I move on with hope and proudly continue to look for only true selfless love."

I took a glance at the clock that was on the wall and realized I didn't have much time left. So I said, "There is a lot to talk about and not much time remaining, so I want to wrap up. Well, ladies and gentlemen, nothing can guarantee success when it comes to finding love. But if you to leave with only one message, I hope that message is that true love starts with you. True love is something you practice over your whole lifetime in order to be able to put aside your own ego and sacrifice and compromise for your beloved. In doing so, your souls flourish in a sacred harmony. So realize that apart from searching for your beloved, a significant part of the process of true love is internal. If you internalize a scared respect for true love in your mindset, then the good habits follow and you are less likely to commit the three forbidden T's of love."

Next, I walked closer to the edge of the stage and said, "Well, I wish I could explain in more details, but my time is over. It seems that there is a short break scheduled for now. I'll be around if you have any questions or just want to say hi. Thank you!"

I wasn't expecting it at all, but I got surrounded by tons of people during the break, some voicing their disagreement and some encouraging me, but mostly asking lots of questions.

After fifteen minutes or so, the break was over. A lady was calling the crowd to come back and take their seats in the hall for the next part of the workshop. The crowd gradually left the break area. As they were moving one by one to get back to their seats, the image of a familiar woman appeared between the crowds. On the first glimpse, she looked like a Muslim girl, wearing Hijab and conservative clothes, but colorful and beautiful. The girl was looking down, avoiding eye contact, so it was difficult for me to see her face well. She was standing towards me with one hand in her pocket and the other holding her purse. I thought she had a question but maybe she was too shy to ask, so I approached her and took a closer look.

My eyes could not believe what they were seeing. Was it Lila?! Here?! In Houston?!

CHAPTER TEN

I stepped a bit closer to her and asked in disbelief, "Lila? Is this really you?"

She slowly looked up to my face with a shy look. It was her with the same shining eyes. She responded in Arabic in her warm voice, "Yes Hadi. It is me."

If I say I was dying out of joy and confusion at the same time, I am not exaggerating. Well, maybe a little bit exaggerating, but the point is I was thrilled to see her! It had been about four years that we hadn't seen each other. She brought back both the good memories of our childhood and the bad memories of how I lost her to a rich guy. Anyway I felt like jumping up and down and hugging her, but in the culture we come from, a guy just shouldn't hug a Muslim lady unless they are family. It's considered rude to someone who believes in that religion, and Lila, to the best of my knowledge, was always a devoted believer.

"Gosh! You have changed a lot Lila. I don't remember seeing you in anything other than a black Abaya cover. Now your clothes are so colorful! But anyway, I'm so pleasantly surprised to see you!" I said as a way of opening up the conversation. She was wearing a dark blue Hijab with white patterns on it and a light blue scarf and carrying a purse that appeared to be a high-quality designer one, which was quite a shift from the Abaya she used to wear in Saudi Arabia.

With a beautiful smile, she said, "That's true, Hadi. I've changed a little bit. I mean, I used to be very traditional but it took me some time to realize that Islam didn't really force women to wear a dark and depressing Abaya. As long as you are modestly covered, it's fine in the eyes of Islam. Time taught me that faith is something you find in your heart more than it is about what you wear."

I said, "We obviously have a lot to catch up. Do you want to grab some coffee and chat?"

"Sure! Only I have to leave soon," she said in a vaguely worried tone.

There were still coffee and bagels left from the break. We got our share and sat down to talk.

I couldn't wait to ask, "So Lila how did you end up in Houston? How long have you been here? What brought you here to this workshop?"

She giggled and said, "A few years' worth of questions right there!"

We both laughed to that. Then she said, "It's not a very long time since we moved here to Houston—five or six months ago, give or take. You remember Ahmed, my husband, right?"

I nodded my head as a sign of affirmation.

She continued, "Yeah, I don't know if you remember, but Ahmed is an executive officer for a government-based oil company back home. They are trying to expand their business in Houston to have office presence in America. We were sent here for his one-year mission. I can't deny it's been a bit difficult for me to be away from my mom and family. I haven't been here long enough to make good friends either, but there's a mosque near our house that I go to for both prayer and socialization. A week ago in the mosque, I saw an advertisement about this event, which led me to this workshop. I had no idea I would see you here."

I said, "Yeah, funny how destiny works. Small world, isn't it?"

She said, "It is. I heard your speech. It didn't surprise me at all. You were always a gentleman even when we were kids. When you disappeared from my dad's house, I wondered where you went. I asked your mom and she told me soon after you left that you had gone to America to get a Doctorate degree. Are you still a student?"

I said, "Yes, Lila. I'm in my forth year. Hopefully soon, I will defend my doctorate thesis and finish the whole thing, but enough about me—how is your mom back home?"

She said, "Everyone's good. Your mom and dad were doing well too. They are very proud of you. Your mom is still a great help to mine. My mom had a terrible lumbar backache recently before I came to America, but thanks to the care your mom took of her, she got much better."

I said, "It's great to hear she is better. Yeah, your mom was really kind to me and my mom. If it wasn't for her, a lot of great things in life may have never happened to me, so I owe her a lot."

She said, "By the way, I really liked the concept of the three forbidden T's. I bet it's your own made-up phrase, isn't it?"

I laughed and said, "Yeah, it is my own artifact of a phrase. And thank you, I appreciate it Lila. How is your life? How is it going between you and Ahmed?"

She fell silent and dropped her head down.

I felt like my question somehow uneased her, and that wasn't at all my intention. It was just a question out of curiosity, so I said, "Sorry, I didn't mean to be nosy."

After a couple of seconds of silence, she said, "No, you are not nosy at all, but you know our culture, Hadi! You know how it teaches us to keep all issues of married life between man and wife! But you are no stranger—I'm struggling. I hope Allah forgive me for spilling out details about my married life, but I'm at a point where I really need help solving the problems I'm having in my marriage, and who is better than you—both wise and trustworthy!"

At first, it crossed my mind that she should probably see a marriage counselor or something. But I also understood why she was avoiding that. The culture we had grown up in often treats women so unfairly: they don't have the right to vote, they are not allowed to drive, they are usually blamed if they talk about their marriage issues to anyone outside their family, and the list, unfortunately, just goes on and on. I felt I should sincerely offer any kind of help that I could, so I said, "Of course, Lila. You can tell me anything you want. I'll try my best to be of help."

She said, "You remember how it all started. I had not even met Ahmed before. I didn't know who he was, what he looked like, or what kind of personality he had. One day at home, my dad came to my room and said I would have to marry him. That simple! He wanted me to marry him because Ahmed's dad is extremely well-connected to the Saudi royal family. Basically, my dad used me as a tool to strengthen his power and wealth."

I said, "Then why did you marry him Lila? Why didn't you resist?!"

She said with a bitter smile, "Resist?! You know our culture and especially my dad, don't you? Women have no rights, whatsoever. What could I have done? Run away? To where? Plus, I put my faith in Allah. I have complete faith in our religion, and you know that Wahhabi Islam teaches women to obey their dad and husbands as if Allah speaks through them. As a believer of Wahhabi faith, I thought I should obey my dad's wishes, even though it was complete madness, and I did so. I didn't have any other option anyway."

She had a frog in her throat, so she stopped talking for a while. Poor Lila! In the midst of the silence that was ruling our conversation, all those memories of our childhood time, all the innocent games of hide and seek we used to play in her mom's garden, all of those precious laughs of hers, all crossed my mind like a movie one more time. That happy Lila I once knew now had so much pain in her heart, and that was breaking me down inside.

After she got it back together, she continued, "And so we got married. For a while, married life wasn't bad. I sincerely tried my best to give him love and be a great wife. He would take me to the mall and offer to buy the most expensive jewelry, shoes, watches, and stuff. I don't think any woman in the world dislikes jewelry and shoes, but that really wasn't what I needed from him. What I really wished to have was his care and attention and, in one word, love. In the beginning, I thought maybe this was the way he had learned to show his love, and maybe he didn't know any better. I thought time would fix these tiny little things."

She finished drinking her coffee and continued, "Over time though, I think he gradually started to show his true face. It all started with him not coming home for a night or two. I didn't make a big deal out of it although my mind was very uneased by the fact that he didn't come home. I thought perhaps it was just this one occasion. Well, it wasn't. He continued to skip showing up at home every now and then. Even when he did show up at home, he was tired and dismissive."

"This continued for a month and I realized I'd better talk to him. He said most of these nights he was hanging out with his friends from the time when he was a bachelor. I tried to explain that I expected him to be the man of his family now that he was married. His response was that as long as he provided me with food and bought me stuff, he was being the man of the family and whatever he did with his friends should be none of my business. That started our first argument. Every couple argues in their married life. That's normal I guess to have disagreements, but disagreement is one thing and being aggressive is another. During our first argument, he lost control of himself and started to throw stuff at me and break things. Then finally, he did what no other man had done to me before. He slapped me, and that's how our first argument ended. I was shocked. For weeks, I didn't talk to him. He didn't seem to care much, either."

Such a coward, I thought, *Such a coward! A man who uses his manly strength on women doesn't deserve to be called a man!*

She continued, "I had no other choice. I went to my dad

and told him what happened, told him that Ahmed dared to slap me on my face! His reaction?! He just said it was normal in Arabic culture and I should tolerate it. I couldn't believe my own dad was telling this. He said he used to slap his wives too, but after he got older and more mature, he stopped doing that. He just suggested that I adapt and give Ahmed time. So I returned from my own dad's home disappointed, sad, and helpless. I just prayed in the hope that Allah would help me to be strong."

I said, "So did time change things for the better?"

"Not at all!" she answered, "Time only made him more aggressive and more relentless than before. If anything wasn't exactly the way he wanted it to be, he would beat the hell out of me. Each and every single day, it was getting worse. Whether it be him slapping me in my face, pulling my hair, or even outright punching me, he wasn't shy of being violent against me."

She took a sigh while tears were banking in her beautiful eyes and said, "I don't know why Allah is testing me with such a man."

I was on fire! I wanted to catch this guy and show him what it's like to be beaten. I couldn't stand seeing Lila in such state of fear and pain. Tears banked in my eyes for seeing Lila this way, but I was trying to hide my tears. I said only one sentence, "I can't express how sorry I am, Lila!"

She continued, "It gets even worse! A year ago, one day, he came home and after eating dinner and sitting in front of the TV, watching soccer, he casually said that he had been seeing a new girl and he wanted to propose to her as his second wife! One of the reasons I changed my beliefs a bit over time was that I could never get over the fact that polygamy is completely permitted in our faith. At some point, I realized some men have made up some of the rules and pushed it into the religion in order to satisfy their own filthy desires. Allah sees every human as equal. I am not a believer that Allah would allow men to be so cruel and have many wives if they choose to."

"So what did you do when he said that?" I asked.

She said, "What could I possibly do? Reason with him? Argue? Object? No, Hadi! It's enough for me to say anything he doesn't want to hear, and he starts beating me to death! When he said that, I only went back to my room and cried my eyes out for a whole week! That's what I did."

I said, "I'm so very sorry, Lila! I really can't stand to see you in so much distress! I am so sorry."

She said, "That's heartwarming! Thank you. Anyway, he got married to his second wife a year ago. He comes home a few nights of the week. Sometimes he barely seems to notice I'm there, and some other times he beats me to death. Like I said, six months ago, he was assigned to this mission and since polygamy is illegal here, he couldn't bring his second wife here, which was good, but it has also made him more aggressive towards me."

She then looked at her wrist watch and said in a distressed tone, "Speaking of aggressive, I'd probably better go soon. He is an extremely controlling man and if he knows that I went outside without his prior permission, I'm sure he will start a fight over it. I left him a note at home with the address, but I am hoping to be back home before he comes back and sees that note."

I said, "Lila, you know I've always been a firm believer in true love, and not only is this marriage not based on true love, but it's the classic definition of an unhealthy relationship. Perhaps, it would be a good idea to start thinking about divorce now that you are in a free country. I'm not trying to push you into anything, but all I know is that you deserve way better than this."

She said, "Have I thought about divorce? Maybe a million times! A while back, I went to see my dad again. I was very serious about divorce this time, and wanted to finalize it with my dad. He and I talked for hours and hours. He didn't like the idea of divorce at all. He had too much stake in remaining engaged with Ahmed's family. He repeated his same old argument about young Arab men and about how he thought time would change Ahmed as it changed him. He told me some crazy things he did when he was young, and asked me to just give it two more years and at the end, if nothing changed for the better, then he would gladly help me in the divorce process. I accepted it out of respect for my dad and Allah's will."

I didn't think Lila giving time to someone who didn't deserve her was a good idea. Not to mention giving time to an abusive guy like him; that wasn't just a bad idea, that was insane! But I kept that to myself. I wanted to respect her decision, so all I said was "I think Sheikh is wrong."

I knew she had to leave, but I exchanged phone numbers with her, and said, "Lila, I understand the judgmental culture back home, and I respect your decision no matter what it is. But this is America! You have civil rights that protect you in case he gets violent again. Please! Please! Promise me to call the police or call me if he ever again dares to—"

"Allah help me!" she interrupted "If he sees us together, he gets jealous and paranoid again! Allah help me! That is Ahmed there!"

I looked in the direction that she was looking. A short Arabic man with a long beard was approaching us with a face full of anger. Part of me wanted to stay and defend Lila, but the other part was thinking that would only make the situation worse for her after I left. I thought I should leave her immediately, before he got there, so as to not increase his paranoia. I got up and as I was moving away, I told her, "Lila, just remember: you are not alone!"

I moved few feet away to the water fountain and acted as if I was drinking some water. I heard him opening the glass door and entering the building. I was trying to spy on him with the corner of my eyes to assure as much as I could that he was not hurting her. He started speaking to her in Arabic with a livid face but a low, growling voice. The first thing he asked her in the most brutal tone was who I was and why she was even talking to me. It was clear he was picking a fight, but he was watching his surroundings and keeping his voice down so as not to show any sign of violence in public, so there wasn't a role for me to intervene. I thought the most logical decision at that point was to stay away from them. I'd never want to give such crazy guy any excuse to cause more damage to her, so I thought Lila would be safer that way. After a few low, inaudible remarks were exchanged, he grabbed her wrist and took her outside. They left the place while continuing the argument.

I spent some time in the remainder of the workshop, but Lila's tears were haunting me and I had lost all motivation and energy, so I left the building and drove to a nearby grocery store to distract my thoughts by doing chores. After about half an hour, I did my shopping and put the stuff into the car to get back home. It was already dark outside. I didn't get very far, however, before my phone rang while I was driving. I pulled over and answered the phone. It was Lila, and her voice was strained and quavering.

"Hadi! Hadi, help! He is going crazy. 1974 Tahoe King Dr., get here right now!"

I said, "Lila, what's going on? Is he beating you?"

But there was no response any more. The call was not dropped but Lila wasn't on the phone anymore. I could hear her screams and Ahmed's yelling in the background. I dropped the call and immediately called the police to inform them of a possible domestic violence situation.

I wasn't very far at all from the address Lila gave me, but I drove like I was in a car race. I got there in a couple of minutes. At first I thought he was beating her again, but this seemed different. There was no sound of any struggle. The front door was open, so I carefully walked in. I yelled, "Lila? Hello? Lila, are you here?"

It seemed like there was no one in the house. I searched the living room and the bedrooms—no one!

But all of a sudden, I thought I heard a soft voice calling my name. I sharpened my ears. It was her voice, coming from the kitchen. I ran into the kitchen as fast as I could.

It was then that I saw the dream of my life shattered in the blink of an eye. I saw her lying on the ground, soaked in her own blood. That worthless animal had stabbed her and run away. I sat down near her, held her head in my hands and I said desperately, "Hold on Lila, hold on please! It's okay. It's okay."

She had bled a whole lot and the color in her face had faded. As I was holding her head, she whispered my name and asked that I get closer to her so I can hear her. She said, "Hadi, I know I'm not making it out of this. So listen. I always secretly loved you. Always! Forgive me if I never told you."

I held her hand in mine and said, "No Lila, you're going to make it. Just stay with me. Look at my eyes."

I put my lips on hers and kissed her. As our lips touched for the longest two seconds of my life, she closed her beautiful eyes forever. Right in my arms.

I cried loud. I had lost everything. Everything.

A minute or two passed. Police showed up, and of course, seeing me with her body in all that blood, they aimed their guns at me, yelling, "Put your hands on your head! Put your hands on your head!" "Lay down on the ground! Lay down!"

They detained me as a suspect but Ahmed was taken into custody that same night a few blocks away. His clothes were soaked in Lila's blood and he was holding the knife he stabbed her with, running down the street away from the house. A police car which was heading towards the house had seen him a few blocks away and saw enough probable cause to arrest him.

My little Lila passed away in my own arms, and only then, too late, I found out that all these years my love towards her wasn't just one-sided. She loved me too.

Soon the news of Lila's murder was everywhere: on TV, in the newspapers, on blogs, and so on. The court had enough evidence with Ahmed's finger prints on the knife, his running away from the crime scene, and above all, his final confession after interrogations to prove his first degree murder. His well-connected dad back in Saudi hired the best lawyers and even put a lot of political pressure through the embassy, but nothing worked. Justice was served. Yet none of that would bring my beloved Lila back to life.

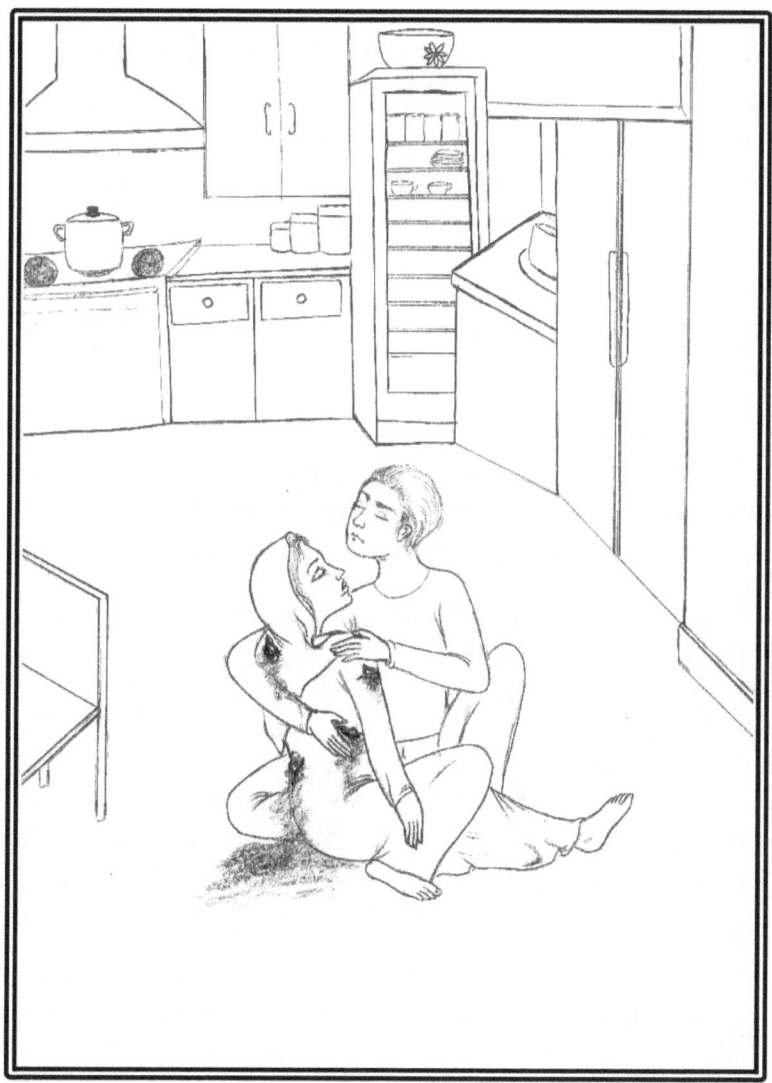

CHAPTER ELEVEN

T his was the last scene I saw under the hypnotic trance. I woke up seeing myself on the same couch I had sat in that morning with Dr. Chapman in front of me. I felt dizzy and numb in the beginning and could hardly move.

Dr. Chapman was scooping some ice cream into a bowl. Offering that bowl to me, she said, "You might be feeling dizzy right now. Eat this ice cream. It helps."

The ice cream I had that evening in Dr. Chapman's office tasted phenomenally good. There was probably nothing special about the ice cream itself, but it was the strangely comforting post-hypnosis feeling that made it taste good, as if my taste buds had become hundred times stronger than before.

After finishing the ice cream, she asked, "Are you feeling better now?"

I said, "Yeah, I actually feel a lot better. I don't really know how this whole hypnosis thing works, but it felt like I was seeing my past like a movie where I was the narrator."

She said, "Yes, that's what is supposed to happen."

But the sweetness of the ice cream soon faded when I remembered the last memory I had seen—the pain of losing Lila, which was the reason I came to Dr. Chapman's office.

Even after about a year since the incident, I had been blaming myself for what had happened to her. If only I wasn't such a coward! If only I had told her how I felt that day I was driving her to her dad's office, perhaps she would be living happily among us today.

How can I speak of love when I was so weak? How dare I?! I was thinking in my head.

I guess Dr. Chapman could read my face, because she said, "But I haven't forgotten you came here to heal a deep wound. You blame yourself for everything that happened to Lila, don't you? But not only that, you are also confused why such awful things happened to you and her despite all good intentions, right?"

I reluctantly said, "Yeah, I guess so"

She said, "I can definitely help you, but I need you to know that this is still your fight. No one can help you better than yourself. I don't have a magic wand to change things instantly."

I said, "Look, after what happened to Lila, I have been visiting one psychologist after another. They all think I'm depressed or delusional. They all judge me by their own presumptions. They prescribe medications that never help even a tiny bit. I'm not depressed, Doctor! Please, whatever you do, don't prescribe more medications! I'm sick and tired of it."

She approached and took the empty bowl of ice cream from me. While putting it on the small coffee table on the side, she said, "Depression? As a matter of fact, dear, I think you are full of life."

She leaned forward a bit and continued, "Do you remember how in your dream, you saw yourself walking in a river between dark and light? That image you saw in the dream is your subconscious mind talking to you, and it has an interesting meaning. Life in general, when you look at it carefully, is nothing but a curious walk, sometimes in the dark and sadness, sometimes in the light and joy. Everyone at some point in their lives has to go through the darkness, which sometimes appears to last so long that we lose hope and think there will never be any light in our lives ever again. We all may feel that way every now and then and that's okay, but what is not okay is to stop fighting. You should never, ever give up on your dream. If you give up on your dream, you will be lost."

I said, "I'm sorry but you haven't experienced the pain I am in, have you? What you say sounds like an empty motivational speech."

She smiled and said, "Neither I nor anyone else could ever guarantee anyone that they will get what they dream of, even if they really want it, but I can guarantee you one thing: You will never get what you want if you stop trying. Hadi, all I'm saying is that the moment you stop pursuing your dream, that very moment you eliminate the chance that you ever see your dream come true. I understand how cold and cruel life can seem when you are walking in the darkness, but if you don't move to your dream, to the light on the horizon, you make it your destiny to remain in the darkness. Does that make sense at all?"

To be honest, that made sense. I immediately said, "But I need guidance to find my way to the light. Can you help me?"

She continued, "I'm here to help if you want."

She sat back again on the chair in front of me and continued, "Dear, the only thing you need is to just move on and continue to follow your destiny. Learn from the past, then leave it behind, and live forward. You need to stop blaming yourself and start to live in the present moment instead of the past."

A tear found its way down my cheek. I said, "Easy to say, isn't it?"

She said, "I'm sure if Lila was to see you in this situation, she would want you to move on and find love, don't you think so? What if what happened was fate and there was nothing you could ever do to change it? What if your true love is out there waiting for you, while you blame yourself for something that was out of your control? Hm? Lila would want you to move on, Hadi! You have a spectacular destiny ahead of you, which is waiting to be fulfilled. That is the message your dreams have been trying to tell you all this time."

I tried to stop tears and catch my throat, but I couldn't stop it. Suddenly, sporadic tears gave their place to sobbing, out loud, from bottom of the heart.

She brought a box of wipes to me, placed her arm on my shoulder, and just let me let it out.

After a few minutes, I stopped crying, cleared my voiced, and said, "I'm sorry. I just couldn't help it."

She said, "No worries, dear. I know how tough it is to lose a loved one. Crying is actually sometimes a good thing. It helps us vent out the old, dirty emotions and makes room for fresh ones."

I said with a calm and low voice, while wiping the tears off my face, "Death of a loved one is one thing and you are right, it's very tough, but what burns me deep inside is the thought that perhaps I ruined the chance we both had to truly love each other. What if she was meant to be my love? What if I destroyed her life and mine by not telling her how I actually felt about her when I had the chance? I blame myself because I feel like I could have saved her life if I wasn't a coward. I feel like I ruined her life, and that's what is really killing me. I speak about selfless love and I really believe in it, but when it was the time to show it, I was just simply too weak! You know what I mean, doctor?"

She said, "Oh, believe me, dear, I know what you mean. But think logically. Is your blaming yourself going to bring her back? Is this going to change anything? No! If anything, it only changes your life for the worse. Your true love might be somewhere out there, and you might miss the chance to meet her if you don't move on with the facts of life. Now am I right or am I right?" She smiled and hoped her little joke would cheer me up.

I remained silent, but nodded my head as a sign of agreement. I took her point.

"This is pretty unprofessional of me, but heck, let me share with you a little about my own life," she said.

She then continued by pointing to a picture on the wall and asked, "Do you know who that man is?"

163

It was the picture of an old guy. I said, "Not really. Is he your grandfather?"

She laughed and said, "No, dear! He is a world-famous nineteenth-century psychologist. His name is Carl Gustav Jung. I told you about Jungian analysis before, remember? Jung's fascination with the ancient art of alchemy led him to found one of the greatest and most profound psychological theories of our time."

I interrupted her by asking, "Alchemy? Isn't alchemy the ancient chemical practice with the goal of turning copper into gold?"

She said, "Yes and no. A lot of people think alchemy is literally turning common earth metals into precious ones, and so did I when I was a kid. I was obsessed with finding the secret of turning metals into gold and silver. I was a strange little girl. I spent a lot of time in my mom's kitchen playing with any material I could find at home and see if I could synthesize the so-called alchemical elixir. Anything I could get my hands on, I would use in experiments—from vinegar and salt I could get from kitchen cabinets, to battery acid I had stolen from my dad's garage. One day, though, it crossed my mind to use electricity along with the chemical reactions I was conducting. We had a radio device, which had an adaptor piece. You know what an adaptor is?"

"Not really," I said hesitantly.

She continued, "An adaptor is a small electronic piece that converts the AC current used in homes to a DC current, sort of like a big battery. It has a bigger part that goes into the socket and a wire with a banana plug at the end. Anyway, I connected the adaptor to the home socket and put the other end into a solution I had made. It suddenly started to foam and the color of the solution changed, which was so cool."

I said, "Wow! You are not going tell me that you found a way to transform metals into gold, are you?"

She laughed and continued her story without directly answering me, "We'll get there, but if nothing else, these experiments had my parents worried for sure. I remember my mom saw me conducting this experiment and she swore at me so much. She said she knew I would eventually kill myself with these experiments, and in response I said, 'Mom, I know exactly what I'm doing.' Of course as a kid, I had no idea what I was doing and those experiments definitely could have killed me if I hadn't used the adaptor with the DC current by sheer dumb luck. But anyway, after a short time, I noticed the other end of the adaptor piece, that is the banana plug which was inside the solution, had turned gold-ish in color from its original silver-ish color. You should have seen the light in my eyes in that moment. I thought I finally accomplished the alchemy many people had failed in for thousands of years. It was a joy not comparable to childish games other kids at my age played. Now it's another funny story how paranoid I became to keep the secret to myself and not let others steal it from me, but let's only say that imagination is a double-edged sword. A few days later, I took that piece to a gold smith nearby to have it tested. He tested it with an acid and immediately told me that it was not gold. As high as my joy was before, now I felt doubly disappointed. Only later in high school, I realized I had only conducted an electrolysis experiment, which had removed the outer silver-ish layer of adaptor piece and had revealed the internal gold-ish blend, which wasn't gold."

I said with a smile to this funny story, "Interesting, but where are you going with this?"

She continued, "After that failed attempt at turning metals into gold, I felt an even deeper thirst—a personal quest per se. Your quest has always been to find true love, and mine was to find the secret truth. I sought eternal wisdom, the mystic forgotten knowledge, the mighty alchemical elixir. I searched the whole world, every country, every province, every little village where I guessed I could find a wise man who would teach me secret knowledge. It took years and years of intense practices in the most remote areas of the world: Tibetan monks, African witch doctors, and South American Shamans, to name a few. But none of those led me to that wholly grail of knowledge and wisdom I so desired."

"It was maddening! Spending almost all of my youth, tons of money, years of bone-shaking training day in and day out, and yet it felt like I had achieved nothing. I tried every possible way, but when it felt like I was getting close to finding the ultimate answer to unlock the mysterious knowledge, it would just simply slip away!"

"Out of absolute frustration, I quit and went back home to England. I had spent fifteen years of my life searching for what I no longer believed in. I felt like an idiot. I felt like I had wasted my whole life following that dream. It felt like I could've been better off in life if I had acted like everyone else, following the crowd. I went back to England and found that all my friends had gotten married; some even had children of their own. I can't emphasize how horrible I felt for following that inner voice that told me my destiny was to search for mystic knowledge."

"For a year or so, I was miserable. I started dating someone, pretending to forget the past, but that deep internal voice did not stop haunting me. I knew it was real. I knew I was meant to be a seeker of truth, but I just didn't know what else I could do. I had tried everything, or so I thought."

"But one day, out of the blue, everything suddenly changed when I least expected it. I went to a bookstore to find a cookbook, but instead I found a book explaining the psychological theories of Carl Jung, the famous psychologist and mystic. I read the entire book in one night. It was fascinating!"

"Again, by what appeared at the time to be sheer chance, the author of the book came to my city to give a talk and I happened to be in the right place at the right time to meet him. After he was done signing books for the audience of his speech, I got to talk to him. In that short conversation, everything clicked. Every word he said opened the door to the promise of the knowledge I had been seeking. Suddenly, I was discovering the ultimate key to the knowledge of the soul. It was amazing, like a moment of pure freedom. He was a master of Jungian psychology from Switzerland. Soon I bought a ticket to Switzerland and started to train under him."

"His training was not based on mystical knowledge or magical powers, but on the knowledge of the self and soul, which I now know is the true mystical and magical knowledge. It took me all those years to realize this, but I finally did. So in a way, I had found the secret to alchemy. Jung concluded that early alchemical masters had chosen a symbolic language, but what they really meant was the transformation of raw human soul into something more valuable. It is very unfortunate that many people are not familiar with Jung's groundbreaking work. Anyway, you may be wondering why I am telling you all these details. Well, just like me, Jung had searched for many years to discover the greatest secret of alchemy: the philosophers' stone! The philosophers' stone was a symbol for the key to turning the human soul into a deeper and more beautiful being. Over thousands of years, many had spent their entire lives searching for it, but had gained nothing; however, Jung was able to find it!"

I interrupted her again, "Wow! Then what is it?"

She smiled wisely and said, "It is love! It is true love, dear!"

She paused for a few seconds and then continued, "Love, when it is real and deep, can transform the raw human soul into something beautiful. It can transform the shadows of the soul such as greed, jealousy, and dishonesty into pure and beautiful spiritual assets like honesty, loyalty, and above all selflessness. I know you are tired and lost; I know you feel you are surrounded by shallow people who want to judge you by your appearance and not the internal assets you have gained, but I want to ask you to be proud of the path you have taken and continue on it because one day, you will find her."

I liked what she said. It felt good to hear that I was not alone in thinking that true love was the secret in transforming human soul. I asked impatiently, "I appreciate that you understand me, but I'm still lost."

She continued, "You have surely noticed by now that my techniques are nothing but unconventional. I see the very core

167

of my patients' souls, so I can tell them things about themselves that they might not even be aware of. I have come to realize that my ultimate destiny is to help lost people find their way back.

Now dear, I can see the uniquely glimmering beauty of love in your heart. I personally admire the values you have stood by during all these years and your wholehearted commitment to love! The fact that you have already realized so much about love means that you are an exceptionally wise man."

"I also see how lost and frustrated you feel. I see how you blame yourself for not being courageous enough to tell Lila you liked her when you had a chance, and how you blame yourself for not being fast enough to save her when she needed your help. I see that heavy burden in your soul, and I understand how painful it is."

"The first step is to forgive yourself for all the mistakes you have made. We all make mistakes. Mistakes are an essential part of life; they give us the opportunity to learn and grow as people. You should realize all the failures of the past say nothing about you as a person. You should realize that destiny sometimes puts you in the complete opposite of what you are, just to teach you what you are not. In your case, for instance, destiny has put you in contact with people who seem to have no clue about true love for the purpose of teaching you what love truly is by showing you what it isn't. You are attracted to what you sincerely wish to be. Sometimes it's straightforward and you get attracted to what you sincerely desire, but also, sometimes your subconscious attracts you to the opposite of what your conscious mind desires. In this process, your subconscious is helping you to purify your deepest desire even more so that you deserve it more once you find it."

"In my case, for example, that entire search for magical powers and mystic knowledge was put in my life for a reason; that is, to eventually realize it was not the knowledge of the outside world that I really sought in my heart, it's the knowledge of the inside. I was looking in the wrong places. It took me ten years to realize that, but my subconscious eventually led me to it. Now I feel happy and fulfilled. In your case, you obviously have already figured that true love is your destiny. But if you compare the depth of your current understanding of love with the understanding you had as a teenager, you will see how all of those failures have purified your love and shown you exactly what kind of love you want. Does that make sense, dear?"

I said, "Actually, it does! This long journey of finding love not only has deepened my understanding of it, but it has made me appreciate that love even more once I find her. It has made me realize that love is everything to me. It has made me realize fear has no place when love is there. It has made me realize love is different from a spark of attraction, or an exchange, but the path to this realization was through all those failures. It totally makes sense now."

She replied with smile, "Yes, dear! The point is that there is a plan in our lives when it comes to the things our heart deeply desires. It's very important for the rest of your journey that you understand this process. Knowing this will help you appreciate all of those failures or difficult situations, because they all helped you to become aware of your destiny. Not only that, but becoming conscious of this process helps you to not blame yourself too much for occasional mistakes you might make in spite of your best intentions. This is one of the things you need to work on, dear."

I nodded my head.

Suddenly, she became abnormally quiet. For a minute, she was just staring at the corner of the ceiling without even blinking. It was bizarre. I was getting worried if she was okay, so I called, "Dr. Chapman?"

She raised her hand as a sign to ask me to be quiet. Then, she looked at me and said, "You know, I just had a revelation. You should write the story of your life in a novel and invite people to that egoless love."

I said in a surprised voice, "A novel? Me?!"

She continued, "Yes dear, you should write a book and put your thoughts about love in it. Has it ever crossed your mind that perhaps your destiny is to be a defender of true love in the time that love is most abandoned? Has it crossed your mind that you should spread the word? I think all of your dreams are trying to tell you this. I think that is your destiny to fulfill."

She continued, "By promoting the wisdom you have towards love, you are serving it. You know better than I do that true love is sometimes seen as an outdated concept in this materialistic world we live. To many people, everything is about money, luxury, and looks. But the type of love you are after is deep and sacred. Stand up fearlessly for that pure type of love. Lead the change. Will you?"

Although the idea of writing a book sounded scary at first, on a second thought, I felt really good about it. There was a deep voice inside me that was saying this was the right move. True love had always been the most sacred voice in my heart and now I could have an opportunity to share that voice with many others through a book. I said, "You know what? On a second thought, I think this is actually a great idea."

She smiled and said, "Brilliant! Yes, I think writing this book will bring many blessings to people's lives."

She continued, "But before you start that, I think you'd better relax for a while. You have been focusing for so long on your failures and the negative experiences you've had that they have caused you to go into a downward spiral. This means that you become more negative internally, which causes you to do things like isolating yourself, which only increase that negativity in your life. In my experience, the key to coming out of any downward spiral is to cheer up. What it means is for a limited amount of time, you need to forget about what you have focused on and just do things that bring you joy, which will relax your subconscious. When you do this, you'll see that everything else simply falls into place. What hobbies do you have? Or what do you do if you want to relax?"

I said, "Uh, I like doing blues and swing dancing. When I'm dancing, it feels like I'm communicating in the language of love without even saying a word. So that's one thing. I also really like nature. I used to sit by a pond in a park near my apartment and that used to make me feel really relaxed, but I haven't done that for a long time, now that I think of it."

She said, "How about exercising? There are scientific studies that show physical activity can bring joy and eventually soothe the mind. You need to exercise!"

I said, "Actually, I haven't recently. I used to play soccer with some classmates at the start of the first semester, but then everyone got busy with courses and we all kind of scattered."

She said, "Those are great. Another thing that I think could potentially help you is what I call compassion meditation. It might sound funny but it has helped lots of people before and I think it will help you too. I'll give you a self-learning book which will teach you, in a simple way, how to use these techniques. It's pretty straight forward."

Then she got off the chair and walked towards her book closet. She took three books off the shelf and handed them to me, saying, "I want you to have these three books. It will help you in the remaining of your journey. This first one is a book about compassion meditation. It helps you stop blaming yourself and move on from the trauma you had experienced. You may use it also to help other people. The second book talks about the different psychological traits that leads to human misjudgment. People seem to pay lots of attention when picking a can of beans at the store, but when it comes to choosing a person to love, they are less aware of the psychological affects and misjudgments that can lead to poor decisions. I hope you can use the content of this book to help people choose their relationships more conscientiously. The last book is about how to write a book. Writing a book helps you to deal with the bad experience and also organizes your thoughts on love. So overall these three books will give you three different tools. I'm sure you will use them well."

I said, "Thank you so much. When should I return them to you?"

She said, "Oh, no worries dear. Next time you see me, otherwise keep them or pass them along to someone who needs them more."

It was already late and we had been doing this one-day session since morning, so I thought it was time to go. Plus, I felt I had found the answer I had been looking for. I was more decisive than ever. I wanted to start writing the book and promote the idea of egoless love as opposed to the spark, exchange, and fear mindsets. If I could help even a single person, I would feel like I had accomplished a huge milestone.

So I thanked Dr. Chapman and left the room. Right before closing the door of her office, she said, "Mr. Shamsi? One last word: You have come a long way to make your dream a reality, so don't ever give up on it. It's not always easy to find that deepest dream of your heart, but once you do, you should never ever let it go. Remember that it's always the darkest before the dawn. One day, you will find your true love, and you know deep in your heart that is worth all the failures and pains you have gone through."

I said, "You are right, Dr. Chapman. Thank you! Really, thank you!"

She said, "I wish you the best!"

I closed the door and left her office to go home. That night, I was exhausted and fell asleep pretty quickly.

The next few days, I thought a lot about everything that Dr. Chapman had said and taught me. Visiting her had not reduced the pain of seeing Lila die right in front of my eyes, nor was I immediately feeling any different than before, but one key thing had definitely changed. I had regained hope: the hope that perhaps there was a bigger plan—the hope that I would find my love one day, the hope that perhaps I was to serve true love by promoting it and supporting true lovers. Yes, hope was once again reborn in my heart, like a shining light with which I could fight all the darkness life had brought to me.

Dr. Chapman did not give me an easy quick fix. Instead, she looked into my mind deeply and reflected on what she saw, like a mirror. She acknowledged that the only one who could help me is myself, but she gave me the insight and guidance of a true savior, and for that I am always grateful.

No doubt, it wasn't an easy job, yet slowly but surely, I started to clear my mind of the dark and sad thoughts and found back the essence of life within. Simply put, I just needed to internalize the fact that the past is past, and no amount of blaming myself would ever change anything; I just needed to realize that I should keep on believing and hoping and working hard for my dream of true love. The rest is looking forward to what future holds, and this was the beginning of my recovery from the trauma.

Per Dr. Chapman's suggestion, I focused on my studies and well-being for a few months without thinking too much about love. Thanks to working hard in my studies, I defended my PhD thesis and even found a decent job as a researcher. At the same time, I made the effort to routinely keep on exercising and doing things that I enjoyed, like hiking and dancing.

This strategy worked. After few months, I was feeling a lot better and perhaps ready to start my new endeavor—that is, to write this book and serve as a humble chevalier of sacred egoless love.

As I had guessed, writing a book wasn't easy at all. It's one of those things that might sound easy– it's just bunch of words, right? But when you actually want to do it, then you'll appreciate how much effort goes into writing a book. It took me more than two years to write the final version you have been reading, but finally, it was done.

I chose to write it in the format of a fictional story based on true events of my own life. It had to be based on the true events of my life so that people would know that the message is genuine, but I also had to avoid using real names and sometimes real locations because of legalities or other limitations. Fiction is not a bad thing, after all. Imagination makes many things more interesting, and it was essential to me that this book would not be read as a dry, philosophical discussion about love, but rather as a true journey with a very important message.

CHAPTER TWELVE

This chapter is divided into two parts. In the first part (Section 12.1), there will be a summary of the four fundamental relationship mindsets. In the second (Section 12.2), I introduce the reader to an exciting practical solution to finding a compatible partner with an egoless mindset.

Section 12.1) Why do many romantic relationships become dysfunctional?

There is probably no need to refer to statistical data to know that many of us face huge problems when it comes to our romantic lives. These problems are not limited to certain cultures, nationalities, or socioeconomic statuses, but truly global issues. Not only are divorce rates still rather high compared to the decline in the number of marriages,[1-3] but also in many cases, the quality of romantic lives may not be ideal at least in certain areas.[4-5] Quite often, romantic relationships of our time start with a cocktail of passion, fear of failure, and materialistic needs, then eventually devolve into a constant battle for control. After some time, all the fiery passion goes away, and the couples think the magic is gone without it. As a result, they seek control over each other, start to cheat and find those feelings somewhere else, or just get out of the relationship to regain what they call freedom. Yet, many others are afraid to even admit the existence of problems in their romantic relationships and pretend everything is fine.

I believe we can do better. I believe we can all find the path to true love. We just need to believe in ourselves, think independently, and walk the less-traveled path. But in order to discover what real love should be, let's look into answering a key question—that is, why do so many relationships fail?

Now, this is a very hard question to answer if we focus on the superficial reasons, simply because there are so many of them. However, we are all human and I think I can safely assume that we have a lot in common. This common ground becomes firmer when we look closer at the root of the human behavior, which is our mindset. Therefore, I tried to find the cause of our relationship problems in our deeply embedded mindsets. Our mindsets lead to our behaviors and usually, they are embedded deep in our subconscious.

So in order to determine why relationships fail, I took a different approach to see why we start relationships in the first place. In other words, I tried to determine what mindsets we build our relationships on. If the foundation of any building is not strong, the taller the building becomes, the more likely it is to fall apart.

Scores of researchers have studied dysfunctional romantic relationships.[6-7] The conventional wisdom suggests solutions that aim to improve partners' ability to communicate effectively.[8] Although I believe these communication techniques are really useful, I don't believe it is the real root of our romantic problems. My hypothesis was that the root cause of our romantic problems is in our mindsets. In many cases, even the best of these communication techniques only help as remedy and not cure to the root cause, the same way a cold relief medicine only provides remedy to the symptoms of influenza for a limited time and doesn't kill the virus.

In order to look into the mindsets governing romantic relationships, the first step is to be conscious of our thoughts. However, many of us do not know why we fall in love.

Sometimes we are fearful to dig deeper because the reasons we love someone may not look so glimmering. So that makes us more comfortable with starting relationships without really knowing why or how it happened, and for a lot of people out there, this intellectual numbness is in fact part of the magic they seek in love. This way we feel good about ourselves and our relationships for some time, but eventually the face of truth shows itself and things may get ugly. Our subconscious mindsets towards love dictate who we fall in love with, but not all of these mindsets necessarily lead us towards true love.

I believe we can all unlock our tremendous potential for true love by identifying these mindsets, analyzing them, purifying them, and hopefully changing them for the better.

At this point, I encourage you, the reader, to pause your reading, and write down your thoughts on what makes you love someone in a romantic way and not love another? What desires or needs are you expecting a relationship to fulfill? What fears make you start or end a relationship with someone? How has it worked out for you? Do you think love is possible without the magic of that initial spark? Are you open to changing your mindset towards love? Grab a pen and a piece of paper and write down your thoughts.

My hypothesis has been repeatedly confirmed that our subconscious mindsets are the roots of many of our romantic problems, and until we fix them, any other solution might be only a remedy, not a cure. Some of these mindsets are put in our heads during the very early stages of our development as children. These mindsets subconsciously influence us to fall in love based on criteria that often don't lead to a true selfless love. A cliché example of this would be the Disney princess movies that girls adore as kids. How many girls do you know who, since a young age, fantasize about a tall, handsome, and powerful prince who rides a white horse and saves them? Except the white horse of our day and time is a fancy sport car and the prince is a tall and handsome alpha-male.

Even if we are not conscious of our mindsets towards love, they do guide our behavior. The majority of people seem to seek romantic partners to instantly gratify their needs, abate their fears, or drown themselves in a sea of fantasies. This is what the majority of people of our day and age call love! I hate to break the news to these people, but this type of love has an expiration date. This is the type of love that might leave you lost and broken. There is a small chance you may get lucky and find true love even with the wrong mindsets, but that is a rare exception. For most people, the beliefs upon which the relationship is based will determine its fate. Such relationships begin with infatuation—which they call love—and end with fights for control, manipulation, cheating, financial loss, and most importantly a broken heart that requires healing over time.

However, we shouldn't blame love for our failures. The problem is that we have forgotten what true love is and put our faith in false ideas about love. We seem to have forgotten that true love is not an exchange, or an escape from our fears, nor a spark of emotions. Perhaps under the constant bombardment of the media, we have forgotten the core of true love; that is, true love isn't just an emotion nor a single action but a deep commitment to a lifestyle of egoless giving. People often don't look for true love even when they think they do. Consequently, they don't find true love, but only a shelter for their fears or a market for the exchange of needs and desires.

My first main purpose in writing this book was to remind people what mindset leads to true love and what doesn't. I intended to inform the audience of this book about the subconscious mindsets that govern our romantic relationships, especially that of egoless love. Without true belief in the mindset of egoless love, it is improbable to reach true love. When you truly believe in the egoless mindset and put your belief into action, you'll see it is not the destination that matters, but the joy that comes with every second of your life along the way. Egoless love is a journey that purifies your soul and makes you a better human every day. I understand this may sound cliché to some, but you'll be surprised to see how impactful it is when firmly believed and constantly practiced.

What I hope to achieve is for the reader of this book to perform a bit of soul searching. I hope the reader looks at their own behavior in seeking relationships and honestly evaluates where those behaviors come from. I hope the reader realizes how taking control over our mindsets can lead to finding a relationship that is not based merely on instant gratification, but rather something much more valuable, true, and pure.

My research has identified four key mindsets that we tend to build our romantic relationships upon. In the rest of this section, I plan to go over each of these four mindsets and explain how we can select the wrong person if we focus on the three selfish mindsets when choosing. As I explained before, this seems to be a common problem amongst many. Of course, the goal of this book is not to force people into giving up their mindsets and choose the mindset of egoless love. The process of altering a subconscious mindset is a gradual one that requires time and practice and can be painful, and a lot of people, unfortunately, choose easy over right. To these people, I admit it is their life and their decision. Also, I admit that all of these four mindsets may coexist together to some extent.

This book is not meant to encourage you to fight against your own subconscious. What I do suggest is to take control of your own subconscious mindsets. I don't deny we all have fantasies, fears, and needs, but a true seeker of love should only let a relationship form if it is based on mutual egoless love, and not on any of the selfish mindsets. In other words, I suggest that the decision of whom you fall in love with should be an intentional choice made based on egoless love, and this can only happen when you don't let your selfish mindsets take over your decisions.

I sincerely don't mean to judge anyone, but my notes will be very honest and frank. If we want change for the better, we should be honest about our shortcomings and welcome constructive criticism, don't you agree?

Now let's look into what those four love mindsets are and why choosing your partner based on them can prevent you from finding true love.

Section 12.1.1) Mindset of Spark

A spark is the special sensation you feel when you see one or many of your fantasies gathered in another person. The sparks can be physical, behavioral, verbal, occupational or many other shapes and forms. They can also be either conscious or subconscious.

Usually, such sparks have a short life span ranging from a night to a few years. Sparks make you feel warm and fuzzy. You may even see the world as more beautiful and poetic when you let yourself fall for those sparks. Although they are usually associated with qualities that would appear shallow from an outsider's perspective, they could feel like deep emotions to the person who is feeling them. Sparks are not necessarily the stereotypes of shallowness, but they can be any fantasy that is not really a true value in a strong relationship. Sparks widely vary from one person to another and there are probably as many versions as the number of humans, but there are still common themes. Apart from physical body type, which is a common spark, another example is when a certain accent is preferred over others. In the long run, it is absolutely irrelevant what type of accent your partner has, yet some people are wired to find certain accents irresistible.

Allow me to clarify once more here: I have nothing against sparks in a romantic relationship, nothing at all. I think sparks are fantastic feelings, but what I seriously warn the reader about is the spark mindset. That is, choosing your romantic partner primarily based on sparks or avoiding others primarily based on lack of sparks. You are following the spark mindset if you only consider dating someone with whom you feel a spark.

The spark mindset seems to be one of the most common mindsets based on which people find a partner, especially in more modern societies and among younger adults. Not only that, but also Hollywood-inspired media is promoting this mindset through their productions. In fact, the spark mindset is often wrongly advertised as love itself.

There are many problems when we choose our romantic

partner based on sparks. One problem is that we all change with time. Not only do our physiques change as we age, but even an unexpected accident can change what you love about the physique of your partner. People also change in terms of emotions, hobbies, habits, and behaviors over years. These changes happen in the partner who fulfilled many of your fantasies, but also, you yourself change. Your desires and preferences change, so how do you know you will still have the same sparks in the future? Life has many ups and downs and change is inevitable in our lives. When change takes those sparks away or you develop a taste for a new type of spark, the relationship based on sparks is likely to be over.

Another problem with the spark mindset is its selfish core. If you fall in love based on the spark mindset, you have truly fallen in love with your own fantasies and not your romantic partner. The kind of relationship that is initiated by the spark mindset often starts out romantic with a melodramatic twist, like the ones we see in the movies. But over time, all the sweet aspects of the relationship gradually or suddenly disappear and what is left is the selfish core. That is what many people refer to as losing the magic. Once the magic is gone, the underlying selfishness encourages the partners to seek control in the absence of the sparks they once had.

Also, despite what they show us in those romantic Hollywood movies, the spark-based love is not really that deep. Certainly, sparks may feel great. In fact, science has proven the chemicals released in our brain on a spark-based love are very similar to street drugs like cocaine. Dopamine, serotonin, adrenalin, and oxytocin are the major chemicals that are released in our brains when we first fall in love. Spark-based love is nothing but another stimulant for your brain chemicals.

When you follow a spark mindset, you are, generally speaking, more apt to be taken advantage of by the playboys or playgirls of the world. To my surprise, there are services out there that teach people how to fake love! They are taught how to abuse the power of psychology and play with others' emotions in order to get laid. The emotional pain that you experience when someone takes advantage of you might stay in your subconscious for years, even damaging your future relationships.

But perhaps the biggest problem in following the spark mindset, as it is with the other two mindsets of fear and exchange, is the lack of focus on the truly important human values of your partner. When you focus too much on finding someone who embodies the fantasies your heart desires, you may reject those who don't immediately show those sparks. You may also neglect to consider some of the more important qualities of the people you do date, the most important of which is selflessness. Many issues that happen later on in a romantic relationship can be traced back to those early decisions. It is futile to think you can go for those sparks and then later change the person to adapt those human values. Selflessness is not something you can teach others unless they have internalized it.

It's simple, isn't it?

At first, it may seem simple to many people to not follow the spark mindset. When I express these points to people, many agree with me, but it becomes difficult for them to put these ideas into practice. Why is that, you might ask?

Well, often our pleasure-seeking mind fools us into rationalizing what our fantasies dictate to us. In other words, we often fool ourselves and do what we know is wrong. I call this "the heart wants what it wants" syndrome.

One of the most common ways we fool ourselves into following sparks is through the misuse of compatibility concepts. Again, don't get me wrong: compatibility between two people in a relationship is crucial, but only when it comes to real core values. The problem is sometimes people use compatibility as an alibi to manipulate their thoughts and follow the warm and fuzzy yet dangerous spark mindset. An example of good compatibility is when two people are aligned in their positions towards serious life decisions such as having children or not. It does make life easier when you are not in a relationship with a person whose idea of life is extremely and fundamentally different from yours.

However, I have repeatedly observed that the idea of compatibility in core life decisions is often twisted into a shallower idea as a way of rationalizing the need for instant gratification of fantasies. An example of a twisted concept of compatibility is when two people fall in love knowing they both have a common favorite band, or they both were in a place at the same time, and then fool themselves into thinking that this is a sign from universe that they are right for each other.

Section 12.1.2) Mindset of Fear

All human beings naturally have their own fears and that is normal. What I mean by a mindset of fear is when we stay in a relationship out of the fear of being alone or the fear of living without a partner you have grown comfortable with. There are perhaps countless types of fears, so the mindset of fear comes in many forms. Some common examples are when you are in a relationship because you are afraid of how others might judge you if you were single, afraid of financial instability, afraid of being alone, etc. A mindset of fear can sometimes be planted so deep in our subconscious that is hard to recognize when our fears are leading us into a relationship.

Generally speaking, in life, making decisions out of fear often leads to a major point of regret. For example, in forensic science, it is known that anxiety and insecurity not only adversely affect our judgment, but also shade our observations and thought process. Selecting a romantic partner out of anxiety, insecurity, and fear is not an exception to this general rule of life. Often, such decisions will be regretted later on when the cause of fear is gone or temporarily ameliorated.

To those who choose their relationships based on the mindset of fear, it's not always clear that they do so. Fear can be a very subtle phenomenon in our minds that we are not automatically aware of. The mindset of fear can have hidden roots in our subconscious and an individual may need professional psychological therapy to unearth those roots.

One example of a relationship that is based on a mindset of fear is a relationship that relies on dependence or habit. You may know some people who are in relationships simply because they are afraid of ending that relationship either because they are mentally, physically, or emotionally dependent or just are fearful of any change. In answer to a question of why they are still in such relationship, they may say something like:

"I don't know how to take care of myself without her. I need her."

"A bird in hand is worth two in the bush. I'm getting old so I'll just give up on true love and settle."

"I'm used to him. Who knows what will happen if I leave him?!"

And these are just few examples of how we can rationalize our fear-based relationships. As I mentioned before, the mindset of fear can have many different variations and sometimes is extremely subtle.

Once again, I would like to encourage you, the reader, to perhaps monitor your own thoughts, talk with a trusted friend, or leverage expertise of a professional to check if your relationships could be based on fears. There are effective ways to learn how to manage our fears over time.

Section 12.1.3) Mindset of Exchange

Exchange, in the form of barter, is one of the oldest phenomena in the human history. In fact, it is believed to be one of the key elements in forming human civilization as we know it today. Exchange has root in our needs. People exchange anything in the hope of finding what will satisfy their needs better. Hypothetically speaking, if humans had no needs, it is hard to imagine we would bother with any sort of exchange.

However, the mindset of exchange in a relationship will not lead to true love because it sees a relationship as only a means of satisfying some sort of need in exchange for something else. The haves and the have-nots that become subjected to such exchanges in a relationship can be very different from one person to another. To name a few, physical needs, sexual needs, emotional needs, and financial needs are the most common ones.

Also, the mindset of exchange can vary depending on the dominant culture of each society. In societies that are under financial stress, wealth and power may be seen as the dominant commodity of an exchange mindset. In more wealthy countries, however, it is possible for sexual needs to become the subject of the exchange mindset in relationships. As with many other human behaviors, in reality it is usually an amalgam of different needs that leads to a relationship based on the mindset of exchange, and not just one.

I need to emphasize that I am by no means condemning human needs, nor am I suggesting we should ignore them in a relationship. We all have needs; it is part of being human. But what I am suggesting is that you should not let the satisfaction of those needs become the primary goal of your romantic relationships. It is crucial that we are aware of the subconscious mindset of exchange before selecting a partner. Once the needs are met in an exchange-based relationship, it could become exponentially difficult to move on even when you finally realize this is not true love.

Similar to the spark and fear mindsets, people who follow the exchange mindset may not be fully aware that their relationship is based on it. These mindsets are often embedded in our subconscious minds, but affect every minute of our conscious lives. For example, there is a social stigma against certain types of exchange mindset when it comes to financial needs being the root of it. In such cases, the mind often plays tricks on the person with this type of exchange mindset in order to rationalize the relationship. The mind senses that admitting the exchange of love for financial stability can hurt the follower's self-image, and in response, it tries to find rather twisted ways to hide it or convince itself otherwise. Just like the other two mindsets we previously talked about, the detection of the exchange mindset can be difficult.

But regardless of what needs are being satisfied in an exchange-based relationship, this mindset is not going to lead us to true love. It simply becomes a trade of what you have for what you want; there is nothing spiritually elevating about it. You might ask what's wrong with that, and my answer is nothing.

As I am no one to judge others, I don't dare to say there is something wrong with any of aforementioned mindsets—only that they do not lead us to true love, a kind of love that can uplift our souls. If true love is not what you want, you probably wasted your precious time reading this book anyway. Most people just know in their guts that it is not right to look at a relationship as an exchange. They know something is wrong with it, even if they find that out after some time. But eventually, they realize the emptiness this kind of mindset creates in our hearts. I would like to believe that emptiness comes about in the heart of exchange-minded love seekers because something deep in their hearts tell them they have wasted a true source of human potential; that is, true love.

One extreme example of the exchange mindset would be the playboys and playgirls of the world. At least to some of these people, love is nothing but a sexual exchange. They look at relationships the same way they look at a shoe in a bazaar. Once they are wearing a shoe, they still keep their options open in case they find a better one. Once they are done using it, they discard it and move on to the next new shoe with shine and glimmer. To these people, there is no end to the variety and quantity of sexual encounters they are on this planet to experience. And don't call me a conspiracy theorist, but this mindset is being advertised in many Hollywood movies of this age and time.

But a subtler example of the mindset of exchange is seeking love based on assets that bring you value. The thought process that goes into selecting a partner in this way is similar to that of a farmer buying cattle. The farmer thinks of the milk and meat and leather the cattle will provide and depending on the breading needs in his farm, will decide on which cattle will be selected. Many people look for someone who has what they have not accomplished in their lives. A calculating relationship based on assets can look like an unbalanced car. True love is about accepting each other's flaws, strengthening each other's positives, and accepting that no one ever will be perfect. It is together that you can become closer to a sustainable and comprehensive perfection through true egoless love.

Section 12.1.4) Mindset of Egoless Love

Well, when it comes to putting the egoless love mindset into words, it is not easy to do justice. Egoless love is something that you should cultivate in your soul and the more it grows, the better you realize its meaning.

One way to define the egoless love mindset is to show what it is not. Understanding the contrast between the three selfish mindsets of love (spark, fear, and exchange) and egoless love both in mentality and action is definitely a start to understanding the mindset of egoless love.

Relationships based on the three more selfish mindsets have failed many of us so frequently that it has become very easy to lose faith in existence of true love in its entirety. Sparks go away as time passes and our fears and needs change, and so does the love that is based on them. The cold truth is that it is natural for a self-serving human to cheat when the source of their so-called love is gone. If you put your faith in the wrong person based on the wrong mindset, I'm afraid failure is, sadly, inevitable.

The expression "Love fades" suggests that people have realized over time that any love based on selfish mindsets fades, but the majority of people have given up the idea of another type of love—a much less-traveled one, the egoless love. In fact, many think this kind of love only exists in fairytales.

Now the next question is if I can define this egoless love mindset by what it *is*, rather than what it is not. As I mentioned before, egoless love is one of those things that you should experience for yourself to know it. It is difficult to talk about it or describe it, let alone to define it. But I think egoless love can be best described as a choice that the followers make to commit themselves to a certain lifestyle, full of giving. It is an individual journey. In this journey, the followers of egoless love should master their own egos in a way that enables them to truly become one with their loved one. True love is that secret alchemy that transforms copper of our soul into gold. This sacred egoless love makes you and your beloved the living manifestation of the yin and yang. This is the type of love worth dying for.

But remember, I never said it's easy. Indeed, to truly walk the way of egoless love is a difficult task. It is a far cry from the instant gratification that many seek. Unlike the Hollywood-inspired common perception, this true egoless love is not an instant moment of spark when you see a pretty girl or a handsome boy. It is a process. It starts even before you meet your beloved, during the selection process, and until you die.

Egoless love is not something that one day may happen to you. It is a choice to selflessly be kind, to give your best, to see your romantic partner as the other half of yourself. It is a choice to see your partner as your soul mate. It is a choice to love him/her with all his/her imperfections. It is a choice to love with all you have, whole-heartedly, forever.

But it doesn't work when it is just one-sided. I have a firm belief that egoless love blossoms when it is mutual. That is why it is essential for people who believe in a deep egoless love to seek compatible partners who share this belief. Remember that you can't change people into egoless lovers unless they commit to this type of love on their own. You can't fall in love based on the spark, fear, or exchange mindset and then expect that over time, you can convince your partner to become an egoless lover. It is a decision that your partner must make for him/herself.

Hardships of life cannot fade this egoless love as long as both sides truly commit to it. In fact, this true love helps them solve their problems in more efficient and creative ways because egoless lovers never give up on their journey. They would choose hell over heaven for their love, if need be.

Selecting the right partner based on the right criteria is important for any healthy relationship. If you really believe in egoless love, but then let yourself fall in love with a person who follows the spark, fear, or exchange mindset, you will suffer sooner or later. But when you find someone who truly becomes one with you, your love life becomes as harmonious as music. Not always happy music; you will have your differences, sad moments, up and downs, but you go through all of it wholeheartedly as one.

By now, you may be wondering, "But, Hadi, how do I know if my partner, or my partner-to-be, truly believes in egoless love too? How can I try to avoid dating people who don't believe in true love? I only get to see their intentions after dating them for a while."

And this is why I thought of a practical idea that I sincerely hope will help all egoless lovers of the world. But before I explain it in the following section, I want to let you know that there is no substitute for what I call active patience—being open to getting to know people, communicating intentions and mindsets, yet not acting too quickly. Remember, finding true love is not a competition. When you find someone who is a true lover and compatible with you, then show them love selflessly.

Section 12.2) I am committed in helping Egoless Lovers to find their match, but how?

In the previous section, my goal was to educate readers on the importance of knowing the four fundamental mindsets that modern relationships can be based on, and encourage them to consider the mindset of egoless love. Now, if you are truly committed to egoless love, I congratulate you for selecting this honorable journey and for choosing a lifetime of unconditional giving over instant gratification.

But be aware that like many other journeys in life, the path of egoless life is full of practical hardships and difficulties. It is easy to get bitter and disappointed, like I had become, but it is essential not to give up. Every time you fail, you need to stand up, take a deep breath, and take the next steps with even more determination than before. As you continue to strive for pure love, good things are happening to your soul. Hardships for a good cause purify your soul like a magical elixir, or the philosophers' stone.

Know that there are other like-minded people out there who are genuinely willing to help you. Know that I, with all my imperfections and flaws, am here to not only show you the way but also provide you with the tools necessary for this journey. There are many hurdles on the way that I plan to find solutions to in a stepwise manner.

One of the most common practical hurdles in the way of egoless lovers is finding a compatible partner who also deeply and genuinely believes in the mindset of egoless love. When I look into the story of my own life as an example, I can see that the structures of societies are built to facilitate relationships based on spark, fear, and exchange mindsets, but not egoless love. In other words, if you want to meet another egoless lover, you have to pretty much rely on luck and randomness since there isn't currently any structure that brings people of this mindset together.

In the rest of this section, we will look into current venues where people typically go for dating and see if these venues are providing the appropriate structural setting for meeting people of the egoless love mindset or not. At the end of this chapter, I will introduce you to the first community for egoless lovers, like yourself, where you can find like-minded people.

Section 12.2.1) Arranged Marriage?

In many Middle Eastern countries, including mine, arranged marriage has been a tradition for ages. The most important characteristic of an arranged marriage is that you don't really get to know the person before marriage.

I have yet to come across any convincing evidence that an arranged marriage can work better or worse than a marriage based on spark, fear, or exchange mindset. In other words, if you marry someone you don't know well, the result would probably not be statistically different than marrying someone based on the selfish mindsets of spark, fear, and exchange. In fact, since you don't know the person you are marrying through an arranged marriage, you are letting chance determine your fate.

Section 12.2.2) Activity/Social Dating?

In the modern era, the most common way two people may start a romantic relationship is when they meet at a social event or activity that is of interest to both of them.

The fundamental thought process for this kind of dating is, at its best, compatibility based on favorite activities and fantasies. In other words, many people think the best match for them is someone who coincidentally enjoys the same things. It starts with "Oh my God, we both...!" and the social settings and activity clubs let people fill in the blank.

It is a form of spark you see when someone is very similar to you, and that is fine, but when it is only limited to small and shallow things, then how do you know if that person is willing to love you through an egoless mindset?

As stated before, I am myself a believer in the importance of compatibility. Not compatibility in small and shallow sparks that do not matter in the long run, but rather compatibility in important subjects, most important of which is the mindset. As I explained in the earlier section, true love must be two-sided. In other words, if you want to be an egoless lover, it is essential that you find someone compatible with you, who also believes in the same type of mindset.

There are a handful of social structures that may provide a systematic chance to get to know people around you in a deeper way for romantic relationships. One example is the school/college system. Ideally speaking, people get to be classmates and friends for four years. At that age as a student, if you are not looking for the instant gratification of spark, fear, and exchange, then school can provide you with a social setting in which you are given enough time to get to know other people on a deeper level, at least ideally.

Unfortunately, not all social structures allow you to get to know a person deep enough to know their mindsets towards love. For example, let's say you go to a bar or a coffee house. There are many people around, but the social stigma of stranger danger makes it difficult for you to approach them and just get to know them (the intensity of stranger danger fear can vary from one culture to another). Now, let's say you found a way to open up conversation and the other person is receptive of it. Social convention again dictates that you should start by just chatting casually about everyday stuff rather than your true innocent intention to get to know them (so as not to scare the person away right off the bat). Let's say you can talk for a good whole hour with that person. But you may ask yourself even after an hour, how well do you know this person? At best, you probably know them only on a surface level, but not deeply enough, so obviously you need much more time than just one conversation to know their mindsets and intentions deep down. But the probability of seeing them again somewhere else is low, so you have to ask for contact information. Here is where the stranger danger fears kick in again. Not knowing who you really are and what you may intend to do with their contact information, there is a high chance they don't share their contact info with you even if they like you. How complicated a simple human conversation has become!

Now, another common perception is that the best way to meet people to start a relationship with is by joining groups of people who enjoy the same activities or interests as you. There are many different social structures that gather people around certain hobbies, interests, or even professional goals. I am not totally against the possibility that you may find a chance to get to know someone on a deep enough level in such social structures. However, in my experience, social structures that gather people around hobbies, activities, and interests also rarely provide an infrastructure for people to get to know each other deeply and often become a good playing ground for people who possess mindsets of spark, fear, and exchange.

There are many social judgments and norms that you are supposed to follow that do not really let you to get to know people deeply, much less to know their mindsets. Also, many people—especially in the age of technology—don't have the attention span or the courage to expose themselves on a deeper level to others. The key problem is that egoless love is very deep and it is really hard to detect who follows it through many of the usual social interactions we have with people. As such, we all have to rely on luck, randomness, or coincidence to hopefully match us with someone who truly appreciates our love.

Section 12.2.3) Online/Catalog Dating?

In recent years, the number and diversity of online dating websites and apps has significantly increased. In my opinion, online/catalog dating has a few advantageous over activity/social dating, but also many disadvantages.

If you want to meet people as part of an activity or social gathering, it usually requires you to be physically present at the locations that offer those activities. The time and energy needed to commute to these locations really limit the number of people you can meet. It might even be fair to say that it is not possible to be so outgoing that you can meet everyone—even in your own city. On the other hand, online/catalog dating gives you an option to look into a larger number of people without spending a huge amount of time to be social.

However, in practice, online/catalog dating is not ideally structured for people who seek true love. In fact, in my experience, online/catalog dating is merely structured to bring passive income to the owners with the cost of promoting the mindsets of spark, fear, and exchange. The algorithms claim they can find the best match for you based only on the shallow questions they ask. Often in reality, matches find each other based on sparks, exchanges, and instant gratifications. True egoless love needs much deeper knowledge and commitment, and existing online/catalog dating solutions do not generally support the needs of people who believe in true egoless love.

Section 12.2.4) This Book Proposes a Parallel Alternative: Join us in a Community of Egoless Lovers

In this final section, I would like to introduce the global community of egoless lovers to the readers of the book. I want you all to know that you are not alone in your belief in true egoless love. There are people just like you around the globe who have a hard time finding like-minded people, and this community is a great place to find them.

The idea of creating a community specifically designed for people who believe in egoless love mindset brings all the good things about activity/social dating and combines it with advantages of an online platform where everyone from anywhere in the world can join. People should join and remain active because they are genuinely interested in sharing their ideas about true love. By belonging to a community of egoless love and contributing actively to it, you will get to know other like-minded people. Although these people are going to be different in their personalities, life goals, and other important factors, such a community could potentially be a great place to make friendships with like-minded fellow humans—and for some, perhaps even to find their love.

The advantage of joining the egoless love community—as opposed to joining activity-based groups—is that you can get to know people deeply by discussing their ideas about love. In contrast, if you join a rock climbing club for instance, you don't necessarily get to know people on such a deep level.

At the time of writing this book, work is in initial stages of progress. I have created a few online platforms that you can read more about in Appendix A (How to Join the Egoless Love Community). These online channels will be a two-way gateway between me, you, and the other egoless lovers. This book was meant to give you a good understanding of the concepts, and more detailed content will be provided to you via the online platforms mentioned above, or other platforms that might be made in future. We will share everyday examples of relationship mindsets, analyze them, and learn from them. We will also talk more about practical ways we can purify our mindsets to enhance our modern romantic relationships. In addition, we will read and discuss your comments and questions.

In order to avoid boring the reader, I did not share the statistical data that supports my scientific conclusions towards relationship mindsets, and only communicated the conclusions. However, as we all go along, I intend to enrich the scientific studies and continuously discuss them in more depth with my fellow Egoless Lovers.

Our community of Egoless Love will be a live and dynamic one. My services to the egoless lovers of the world can expand over time if the community of people who believe in true love really supports me on this path, but these online sources will always be the starting point to join your fellow egoless lovers. I am very excited and hopeful to make a positive, practical impact in the lives of believers of egoless love.

Some believe true love is like a religion—in the sense that you have to keep your faith in it—but a religion that does not belong to any particular group, race, country, sex, or sexual orientation. They say true love opens the door of Heaven—not in another life, but in this very life—in each and every moment when you let its sacred eternal light shine into your heart. A symbolic light that purifies you from selfishness as long as you humbly keep letting it in. Well, if you believe in the true love I have described in this book, then allow me to be a prophet of that religion for you! Let us bring the teachings of true egoless love to the believers' lives on this small yet vast planet. Some will keep denying; let them deny. But some will follow; let them achieve true love. So join the rest of your fellow egoless lovers in our journey and let the end of my book be the beginning of your story.

Appendix A. How to Join the Egoless Love Community

I am starting small by creating a website and email address where you can contact me directly, a YouTube channel where I will post videos about true love, and a Facebook page where you can post your ideas about egoless love, too. More social media channels may be developed in the future if need be. The electronic addresses of these websites can be found below.

Egoless Love Email (Limited Response)
Although I may not be able to immediately answer every email that is sent to me, this will be the quickest way to contact me, especially while the website may be under construction or repair.

Egoless.love.book@gmail.com

Website
This is the only official website dedicated to egoless love anywhere in the world. You will be able contact us, subscribe to our community, get information about upcoming events, and much more.

www.egolesslove.com

YouTube Channel
Follow the link below, or simply go to YouTube.com and search for my channel, called Egoless Love.

https://www.youtube.com/channel/UCEavfOlL-pkBfJLGfXngZNg?disable_polymer=true

Facebook
Follow the link below, or simply go to Facebook.com and search for my channel, called Egoless Love.

https://www.facebook.com/Egoless-Love-1887320568167468/

Appendix B. Notes

1. "SF3.1: Marriage and divorce rates," OECD Family Database, OECD - Social Policy Division - Directorate of Employment, Labor and Social Affairs, 2018, https://www.oecd.org/els/family/SF_3_1_Marriage_and_div orce_rates.pdf

2. "Provisional number of marriages and marriage rate: United States, 2000-2016," United States Center for Disease Control and Prevention/U.S. National Center for Health Statistics, 2016, https://www.cdc.gov/nchs/data/dvs/national_marriage_divo rce_rates_00-16.pdf

3. "Crude Divorce Rate," United Nations Department of Economic and Social Affairs, Population Division Database, 2008. https://www.un.org/en/development/desa/population/publi cations/dataset/marriage/crude-divorces.asp

4. Carr, Deborah et al. "Happy Marriage, Happy Life? Marital Quality and Subjective Well-Being in Later Life." Journal of Marriage and the Family, vol. 76, no. 5, 2014, 930-948. https://www.ncbi.nlm.nih.gov/pmc/articles/PMC4158846/

5. Spanier, Graham B. "The Measurement of Marital Quality," Journal of Sex & Marital Therapy, vol. 5, no. 3, 1979, 288-300. https://www.ncbi.nlm.nih.gov/pubmed/513146

6. Creasey, G., & Hesson-McInnis, M. "Affective Responses, Cognitive Appraisals, and Conflict Tactics in Late Adolescent Romantic Relationships: Associations with Attachment Orientations," Journal of Counseling Psychology, vol. 48, no. 1, 2001, 85-96. https://psycnet.apa.org/record/2000-14217-010

7. Shulman, Shmuel and Kipnis, Offer. "Adolescent Romantic Relationships: A Look from the Future," Journal of Adolescence, vol. 24, no. 3, 2001, 337-351. https://www.sciencedirect.com/science/article/pii/S0140197 101904099

8. Gary Chapman, The Five Love Languages, 1992. https://www.5lovelanguages.com/

ABOUT THE AUTHOR

Hadi Shamsi is not a traditional relationship guru or psychologist by trade. Rather, he is a scientist who holds a Ph.D. in engineering. He has authored more than 14 peer-reviewed articles in respectable scientific journals and more than 400 independent scientists have used his scientific studies or referred to them in their work. However, Hadi's true passion has always been understanding love—how it develops, how it can die, and how to keep it alive. As can be read in this story, Hadi has personally encountered many ups and downs in his journey towards love. By analyzing these personal experiences, Hadi employs the same cerebral, scientific approach he uses in his research for the purpose of identifying the root causes of our modern relationship problems.